New Strides of Faith

New Strides of Faith

BY Carl F.H. Henry

MOODY PRESS · CHICAGO

Library of Congress Catalog Card Number: 72-77956

ISBN: 0-8024-5917-X

Printed in the United States of America

Contents

Acknowledgments

1. "A Generation on the Go." Commencement address delivered at Judson College, Elgin, Ill., Sunday afternoon, June 28, 1970.

2. "Which Way Is Heaven?" Address at the commencement exercises of Eastern Baptist College, St. Davids, Pa., on Sunday, May 17, 1970.

3. "Putting the Evangelical Witness in Orbit." Syndicated article prepared for Evangelical Press Association in January, 1969.

4. "Christian Theology in a Runaway World." Address given at the Sidgwick Avenue Site, Cambridge, on Friday night, January 31, 1969.

5. "The Future of Religion." Public lecture given in Butler University Chapel, Indianapolis, on Sunday night, February 8, 1970.

6. "What I Think of the Ecumenical Movement." Address to the Ohio Baptist Convention in Youngstown, Ohio, on Friday afternoon, October 17, 1969.

7. "Christ and the Crisis of Our Age." Address given at Singapore Conference Hall at an open meeting arranged by the Graduates' Christian Fellowship in Singapore in November, 1968.

8. "Christ Appeared!" Sermon delivered in the Church of the Holy Sepulchre (the Round Church) of Cambridge, England, on Sunday morning, April 20, 1969.

9. "The Risen Christ and Modern Man." Address to the Kiwanis Club of Philadelphia in Bellevue-Stratford Hotel on Tuesday, March 24, 1970.

10. "The Disturbing Shadow of the Risen One." Address in the Tenth Presbyterian Church of Philadelphia, Pa., on its missionary Sunday service attended also by members of the Eastern Regional branch of the Christian Medical Society.

11. "Sent into the World." Address at the concluding gathering of the Evangelical Fellowship of Canada at the 1971 national convention held in Knox Church, Toronto, Thursday night, March 11, 1971.

12. "The World, the Church and the Gospel." Address to the Ohio Baptist Convention in Youngstown, Ohio, on Friday, October 17, 1969.

13. "When the Doors Are Locked." Address in St. Louis to leaders of the Key '73 program for grass-roots evangelism throughout America.

14. "Is It Too Late for the Church?" Open lecture given in Cambridge, England, on December 3, 1968, in a series on "Christian Advance in Days of Doubt" sponsored by evangelical churches of Cambridge and vicinity.

15. "God Speaks in Renewal." Comments at American Baptist Convention, Cincinnati, on Saturday, May 16, 1970.

16. "The Barbarians Are Coming." Address on Thursday, October 23, 1969, on the occasion of installation as visiting professor of theology. Published in *Eternity* magazine as "What's Next?"

1

A Generation on the Go

OURS IS A GO-GO GENERATION, unsure where it is going. We have become a generation of nomads; multitudes no longer have a sense of home. Big business shuttles its executives from post to outpost, establishing new locations and planting bustling new communities. Air travel puts whole nations in the sky, and 21,000 feet aloft in jumbo jets passengers complain to stewardesses that the food service is too slow. Those gyrating go-go girls are a symbol of our generation perpetually on the move.

We are becoming nomads in the world of ideals and values no less than in the world of space and time. Family roots run sadly shallow; on one campus scores of students refused to go home for the Easter holidays because they no longer respect the values held in cold storage there. In *Gone With the Wind* Scarlett O'Hara tells Rhett Butler, "I've felt as if I were in a heavily loaded boat in a storm and was about to go under; so, I dumped overboard all the things that did not matter." "You are right, Scarlett," Butler says; "pride, honor, virtue, truth, these aren't important when your boat is sinking." That tide of moral relativism and situation ethics is now sweeping over modern life.

We are becoming vagrants in the world of truth. The prejudice grows that logical forms and concepts are merely evolutionary deposits, that all truth is historical and culture-bound, that nothing is permanently true and nothing is always wrong. These notions, like a polluting smog, are settling over modern civilization. The myth is spreading—it has al-

ways had advocates in times of widespread doubt and uncertainty—that there is no absolute standard of truth and
right, that man is necessarily a victim of cultural relativism,
that no judgments hold universal and objective validity. Even
the pagan Greek philosophers Plato and Aristotle fought this
myth as they would have fought a deadly plague, but it has
come alive again to haunt us.

Multitudes of young moderns, trapped in the relativity of
modern life, sense that they are cut off from any real future
and wonder whether the present is any longer worthwhile.
Teenagers by the droves ask whether life holds any real
prospect for them or whether they belong to the apocalyptic
generation. At the end of a planetary development of perhaps four or six billion years, have we bequeathed them a
technological civilization whose pollution may soon poison
the only planet on which life is known to exist? Have we
reserved for them a world doomed to atomic destruction? At
the end of thousands of years of human history have we
destined them to be the generation in which herds of human
beings will climb over each other like ants searching for food?

In Hong Kong I have seen resettlement apartments where
families of four occupy a ten-by-twelve-foot room and share
a communal toilet. A cluster of twelve-story apartment buildings is now rising to house another 120,000 people. The million persons who came there from Red China have already
become four million by natural reproduction. In Singapore
I have seen an apartment complex housing 200,000 persons.
What do such trends imply for the twenty-first century?

Why do multitudes of young people recoil from this world
and turn to drugs to escape it? Why do legions of teenagers
sense that the locust years are upon us? Why do they wonder
whether omnipotent astrological powers are not moving our
generation toward Aquarius? Why does a sense of crisis pervade our modern Eden? Why does the dark cloud of approaching nihilism already hang low over the cosmos?

Because of the hollow history of the twentieth century,

that's why. Man can probe the distant planets but cannot love his neighbor or accept his fellowman of a different color. Communication has exploded into a Babel of twisted meanings, until hate and love are synonyms, war and peace mean the same, and Madison Avenue calls a Winston good. Our generation has computerized more knowledge than we can use; yet we move from one world war to another with ever more lethal weapons.

Not only is this a go-go generation unsure where it is going, but ours is also a go-go-going culture that scarcely suspects it is about gone.

A few months ago I met with twenty-five missionaries back in the United States on furlough from many lands. They served under many denominational and independent boards. All were staggered by the evident decline in American morality since their last furloughs: unsafe streets in the big cities, the rising crime rate, the striking change of mood on the campuses, addiction to drugs, the ready resort to coercive tactics for swift social change. One missionary, on his fourth furlough in twenty-four years, said that the United States has sunk farther between each visit. His feeling was that this nation is going, going, going, and that next time it may be gone. Perhaps you have heard of the airline pilot who unexpectedly came on the intercom system and announced: "Ladies and gentlemen, I have both bad news and good news. The bad news is that we are lost. The good news is that we are ahead of schedule." We seem to be both lost and ahead of schedule.

With President Nixon I agree that there is much that is wonderful about this land and that for our assets we deserve a better press. I never travel about this world but that I return to the United States with gratitude; no soil seems as wonderful to the step as that of America. And despite what is often said about our having an adverse image around the world, most of the people I know in Asia, Africa, and Eastern

Europe, and other places as well, would still give a great deal
to live here among us. Yet, very much *is* wrong with our
country today, and I find nothing in the Bible that promises
the United States a permanent place in the family of nations
or in the history of the world, and nothing that exempts it
from the rule that "righteousness exalteth a nation, but sin is
a reproach to any people."

Only the technological success of modern science masks
the moral failure and spiritual vagrancy that are fast over-
taking our society. Because all signals are "go" at Cape Ken-
nedy, we fail to see that in other aspects American life is
already far "gone." We have drifted so far from our Christian heritage that few persons are any longer aware of the
debt humanity owes to the religion of the Bible. We forget
that nature was once thought to be in the grip of astral
powers and polytheistic gods. Confidence in God the Creator
banished those myths and superstitions and set the physical
world free for the whole enterprise of science.

We forget that kings were once worshiped as gods, and
that kings arrogated to themselves a divine right to rule. The
revelation of Jehovah as Ruler of the nations and of the risen
Christ as King of kings and Judge of the nations stripped
away these pretenses. Then the political arena was loosed
from the ancient myths, and men were free to champion the
will of God against the will of tyrants.

An earlier, more devout generation knew that in its account of the origins of human culture the Bible specifically
notes that in those days "began men to call upon the name
of the LORD" (Gen 4:26). Today the scientific enterprise has
cut loose from the command of God. Technological man considers himself the undisputed lord of nature and arrogantly
reaches for sovereignty over his own future.

The haunting melancholy and the cynical amorality of the
pagan past are creeping over the spirit of man again. Once
the Christian conscience revolted because ancient Romans
exposed their unwanted babies in the open air to die; today

many are tempted to throw them out with the medical garbage. All the spectacular techniques of modern science are being used by the barbarians for destructive ends. Someone has said that this is the first generation to live constantly with the fear that some madman might press a button and bring history to an end.

What a damning commentary our present cultural crisis provides on the liberal theology that decade after decade in the forepart of this century deformed Protestantism and sapped the energy of Christianity. According to that optimistic religious theory, modern scientific and political and cultural developments were to be viewed as the unveiling of God's kingdom. To it, the whole movement of modern history was secretly divine. Liberalism scaled its view of the kingdom to a description of Western European culture. This brand of culture-Protestantism is now drifting to the still more radical extreme of declaring that God is speaking in the revolutionary sociopolitical movements of our time. Because it has forfeited the transcendent Word of God, it is doomed to bow down continually before the cultural agonies of a civilization in distress.

Modern man has cut off the route to meaning in life. While he is making amazing advances in controlling the material world, man remains a moral and spiritual juvenile delinquent. This is his penalty for worshiping science as the sole source of knowledge. On the seal of Harvard University is an open Bible across which is written the word *veritas*. We have lost the Book of books, and we have lost the truth of God. It is not only the truth of the evangel that modern man has lost; he has lost the meaning of meaning and the truth of truth.

The Bible remains God's hot line to this generation. His message has already been decoded and translated into a thousand languages: "Yet once more will I shake the earth," He says; "today if you will hear my voice, harden not your heart."

Although this is a go-go generation unsure where it is going, and ours is a go-go-going culture with not much farther to go, Christians are history's go-go vanguard who know where they are going, and who and what is coming.

"Eye hath not seen, nor ear heard, neither have entered into the heart of man, the things which God hath prepared for them that love him" (1 Co 2:9). That ancient text may well remind us that neither by scientific searching nor by philosophical speculation has man laid hold on redemptive knowledge or eternal life.

The whole point of Christian preaching and Christian education is to make the real existence of transcendent truth and eternal good and final purpose and resurrection power inescapably clear. Their purpose is to exhibit the holy God as the center of the moral universe. They must show that nothing can be placed above the truth and goodness of God. A Russian biology and a Swedish morality and what passes for an American spirituality will fall under divine judgment no less than a Nazi anthropology. Truth and the good do not bear the imprint "Made in America"; any nation that thinks it makes the moral code succeeds only in breaking it. Culture may determine the beliefs and behavior of a given period, but it cannot establish their truth and goodness.

Christian churches and schools are to vindicate what the Bible says as indeed the truth about modern man. They are to remind modern man of the nonsensicality of calling talk about God nonsense and to remind him of the futility of prattling about the silence of God, the absence of God, the death of God, and the burial of God. They must remind man that it is man himself who is dead, man who needs to be humanized, man who needs remaking, man whom God loves. It is man for whom Christ died, man to whom God holds open the future, man whose nature Christ has carried into the heavens, man who can know the forgiveness of sins and new spiritual being and share a life fit for eternity. This same man, who mistakenly thought he could live by telephones and television, by automobiles and airplanes, needs to learn that all his bread turns stale because he fails to live by every word that comes from the mouth of God. Modern man needs to be told that this globe need not wobble out of orbit and that the smell of death can be lifted from contemporary life.

Christians are history's go-go vanguard who know where they are going and who and what is coming. They know that present political processes and totalitarian tyrannies do not represent the apex of power. They know that Jesus the crucified is risen from the dead, that a judgment of the nations is coming, that the King of kings will finally vindicate righteousness and banish evil. They know, too, that even an empire tottering on the brink of the abyss can find repentance and new life if men will humble themselves in God's sight and seek new hearts. They know that even in a scientific age when human nature seems to have gone out of control, Jesus Christ can renew and remake men.

"Go into all the world"—that is the *go*, the momentum, of the Christian movement. This generation still untold, still unsought, still unloved, needs urgently to know that God cares and that God's people care. We must go as did the early Christians. They carried the truth of God to Asians who lived among the ruins of past civilizations, to Greeks whose classic glory had long ago faded away, to Romans who little suspected that their world empire was suspended over a smoldering Vesuvius. We must go to America, the great world power whose predecessors in the same mighty role have all either gone third rate or marched off the map. We must go and tell that what passes for life today is but a living death, that truth and the good are not mere social conventions, and that God's Word and commandment are forever. We must go and tell modern man that *he* is the one for whom Christ died in order that he may be the man God wants him to be.

2

Which Way Is Heaven?

NOT LONG AGO a Mississippi driver about to enter Washington, D.C., picked up an old farmer hitchhiking. "Where are you going?" asked the Mississippian. "Son," answered his new passenger, "I'm on my way to heaven, and I've been going there for thirty-five years." "Well," replied the driver, "if you've been going there for thirty-five years and haven't got any closer than Washington, D.C., I'm not interested."

So, which way is heaven? Where it lies is hard to judge from the traffic of modern life, much of which seems headed in strange directions. Even religion follows an unprecedented course. The emergence of atheism as a global phenomenon is one of the most conspicuous developments of the twentieth century. Once it was the strange ideology of a few isolated intellectuals; today an atheistic theory of life governs many nations once friendly to the Christian religion. In most Eastern European countries, churches now survive by the reluctant tolerance of totalitarian authorities, and Christianity must contend constantly with official atheistic propaganda, pressures on converts, and restrictions on evangelism.

No less important is the decline of ecumenical Christianity into a theological hodgepodge having little missionary and evangelistic vigor. As historian Kenneth Scott Latourette noted, the "century of missionary expansion" crested by the year 1900 in a mighty wave of evangelical ecumenism. Churches almost everywhere, espousing a theology that was then predominantly biblical, were active in transdenomina-

14

tional missionary ventures. Under auspices of the World Student Christian Movement hundreds of young Americans from leading universities moved to distant lands to "win the world for Christ in a single generation."

But an ecumenism emerged whose central concern was organizational and structural. The idea held sway that the world would become impressed with the centrality of Jesus Christ if church members everywhere could be incorporated into one global church. Disunity was considered to be the big sin. The church's task in the world was identified as politico-economic, and enlightened legislation was considered the sure means of transforming social institutions into the kingdom of God.

This trend continues to our own day, except that, unable to achieve its goal by persuasion, Protestant liberalism now often promotes it by a theology of revolution. The nations of the world today face problems far removed from the ones ecumenists projected in the forepart of this century; at that time churchmen envisioned worldwide democracy in a scientific utopia with the example of Jesus Christ as the center of human brotherhood. Today the whole human family is staggered by massive problems, and man himself is the most conspicuous of them.

The predicament of the churches is equally striking. Even Roman Catholicism has plunged into a desperate battle over authority and over celibacy and contraception. Neo-Protestant ecumenism is in deep trouble. Replacing small denominations with larger ones has not brought about one vast church, let alone impressed the world. In England, rejection of Anglican-Methodist merger proposals reveals a waning ecumenical enthusiasm; the very word *Uniting* in the projected Church of Christ Uniting (COCU) betrays as much frustration as actual achievement.

The organized church is under increasing pressure. Christian vitality is slipping from it to new cells and new groupings of believers. Church leaders often try to explain the diminishing financial support of organized Christianity and the ever decreasing church attendance in terms of the strong ecumenical stand on civil rights. But this explanation will not hold. Most college and university students hold firm positive convictions on the issues of race and civil rights, but they care very little about ecumenical Christianity. Many students wonder whether institutional Christianity even deserves to survive, and on many campuses ecumenical student work has all but disappeared. Precisely at a time when the truth of revelation and moral certitudes are everywhere under fire and need reinforcement, the pluralism and tolerance of ecumenical Christianity is militating against absolutes. Influential churchmen claim to speak as Christians and yet stir up tidal waves of doubt about the theology and values of our Christian heritage. The most spectacular renegades theorize that God is dead and that morality is situationally rather than scripturally determined.

Which way is heaven? Today even many church members are confounded, and our generation is tempted to think that spiritual direction is not nearly as important as the reality of this present world. Historic Christianity, or the evangelical faith, has sought to hold the two worlds in balance, and its impact on man's earthly life is clear; almost all modern humanitarian movements had their source in the Christian view of man and life. Loyal to the truth of the Bible and to the priority of evangelism, evangelical Christians form an important vanguard both inside and outside the conciliar ecumenical movement. They are still the largest segment of American grass-roots Protestantism. For them, as for the apostle Paul, the heart of man's best news is "that Christ died for our sins according to the scriptures; and that he was buried, and that he rose again the third day according to the scriptures" (1 Co 15:3-4). Billy Graham best reflects the movement's evangelistic vitality; *Christianity Today* mirrors some of its theological vigor; many evangelical seminaries, contrary to others, have full enrollments. All in all, the evangelical movement continues to be the source and support of most of the missionary task force around the world and of evangelistic expansion at home.

At the same time, evangelical Christianity suffers from isolation and independency. Concentrating their cooperation almost entirely on evangelism, Evangelicals have failed to exert a telling influence on modern culture. Today the way of life proclaimed by Christianity turns off many young people. While Christians speak wistfully of a "new heaven and new earth," the oncoming generation is defining for itself a new "heaven" of a wholly different order.

There is the new "heaven" of outer space to which modern man is becoming a commuter. It not only offers prospects of space travel, but also leads many scientists to suggest that planetization may occur, just as colonization did in the past. The space age sees planet earth in new perspective and has launched modern man into new heavens.

There is another new "heaven" of sex. Fearless experimentation is the popular thing. Teenagers assure themselves they can go all the way without significant consequences, physical or moral, and without assuming marital obligations. In his book *Situation Ethics,* Joseph Fletcher writes: "The civil lawmakers are rapidly ridding their books of statutes making unmarried sex a crime between consenting adults. All situationists would agree with Mrs. Patrick Campbell's remark that they can do what they want 'as long as they don't do it in the street and frighten the horses.' "[1] Now, a moral philosophy sensitive only to horses and streets ought to be transparently bankrupt even to a college freshman. To be sure, the new morality appeals to love, thereby distinguishing itself from an openly relativistic ethic, and provides itself with an aura of piety. But love is not self-defining; moreover, the situational approach disowns universally valid moral principles. One soon gets the impression that whatever one wants to do is all right as long as one loves to do it.

Then there is the new "heaven" of physical immortality. Some scientists envision routinely replacing worn-out parts of our bodies and perhaps "cloning" special genetic types.

This new image of the heavenly—human imperishability, unlimited deployment in space, and infinite sexual indulgence—is the by-product of a scientific and sensate age. Science reduces everything, including the human self, to quantifiable mathematical formulas that swallow up the personal in the impersonal.

Thanks to science, there is even an escape from the tyranny of science in the new "heaven" of drugs. Modern youth turn to drugs in quest of a transcendent realm. They long for a psychic supplement to the quantitative.

The importance of all this is that the present generation is trying to forge a whole new ideal of the good life. Many observers underestimate the crisis of our time by isolating some one problem, such as war, race, poverty or pollution. Important as these are, the deepest problem of the twentieth century is a problem of spirit. What is the essential nature of man? What is the good life? What are the nature and will of God? Alongside these, all other conflicts, however important for human destiny, are provincial struggles. We may wrest some sort of accommodation from Vietnam and abate the racial strife, but if we fail to rediscover who we really are, we shall yet lose the meaning of human life.

Which way is heaven? If the practical utility of the scientific method means we can no longer believe in a transcendent world of truth, if acknowledgment of historical conditioning means all values must now be read on a constantly shifting evolutionary scale, then let us say so and be done with it. Let us not lament the decline in churchgoing; rather, let us join the absentees.

Let us, however, be clear about one thing. In that case, all inherited values and all beliefs about God's will give way, and with this the rationale for transcendent justice. Evolutionary theory can provide no sound basis for universal and enduring human rights. The possibility of a self-appointed superrace always lurks in a merely evolutionary view of life —and the Nazis need not have been the last to act on the possibility. At any time humanity as a whole may be best served by the extinction of a particular remnant, whether it be the Jews as in Hitler's time, or again the Christians as in Nero's day. The only secure foundation for universal and enduring human rights is the dignity revelation gives to man as God's creation. The new heaven of modern times is a gilded hell; the difference is clear to those who know another heaven and true life on earth.

3

Putting the Evangelical Witness in Orbit

EVANGELICAL CHRISTIANITY faces a new opportunity to mold the spiritual temperament of the present age. Despite the liberalizing and ecumenical tendencies that currently dominate the religious scene, a new wave of orthodoxy is widely evident. This fact is apparent not only in the evangelistic momentum of evangelical Christianity, cresting into congresses for evangelism on all continents, but in the arena of thought and learning as well. Today the most vigorous religious groups on college and university campuses are almost invariably the evangelical movements. The theological schools that are drawing large enrollments without substantial subsidy are mainly conservative in theology. This is true not only in the United States, but also in England, where the number of evangelical ordinands to the Anglican ministry has shown a phenomenal increase.

The vascillation in modern theology, with constant turnover of doctrinal wares, has discouraged many from making final theological commitments. But it has also prompted not a few others to turn again to the faith of the Bible. One hears now and again of the conversion of liberal pastors. In the Church of Rome more and more of the laity, and not a few priests, are joining with evangelical believers to assure themselves of the reality of the new birth and of a vital relationship to the Bible. A layman from Puerto Rico recently remarked, "Before I knew my Protestant brethren, my thoughts moved from the pope to Christ to Mary; now they move from the Bible to Christ to the Holy Spirit."

The evangelical resurgence coincides with an immensely important development in the modern intellectual world. Recent efforts to discredit faith in God by declaring all metaphysical assertions to be invalid are slowly but surely grinding to a halt. In Britain the logical positivist's attempt to dismiss metaphysical statements as meaningless nonsense has had its day; not even its central dogma—the verifiability principle—could be validated by logical positivism's own criterion, that of empirical scientific method. On the Continent the dialectical and existential theologies are now also on the wane. Barth and Bultmann surely did not intend, as did positivism, to destroy or discredit faith in God. But, no less than positivism, they denounced all metaphysics and all assertions about the nature of God-in-Himself as sheer philosophical speculation.

The anti-intellectual trend in modern theology gave anti-supernaturalists the whole field by default. Scientists are able to get astronauts to the moon in less time than it takes a mediating theologian to explain what he now means by heaven and hell. While science has opened up new worlds, theology and philosophy have blurred the world of spirit, soul, conscience, reason and truth—realities upon which every great civilization has been built. Small wonder Dr. Edmund Leach in his controversial *Runaway World?* suggests the time has come for the scientist to proclaim himself God. Scientists are to shape a new heaven and earth and to decide who of which species will survive to inherit it. More and more the shadow of "the man come of age," of the so-called "fourth man" or secular man who thinks only in terms of man's powers over nature, hovers over our civilization.

Multitudes, however, are unconvinced that modern science, philosophy, or theology has really opened a window to the ultimate world. Philosophers and scientists may try to wall out the supernatural, but the masses are scrambling around and over the walls. The awareness is growing that for all its legacy in the way of mass media and modern travel and gadgets of comfort, modern science has done little to meet man's deepest needs. Popular faith in science has declined; the perpetual prospect of nuclear war, the barbarism of the Nazi camps, and the shoddy violence on television were all made possible by science.

Some have opted out of modern life and culture. Sentimental interpreters are mistaken in casting the psychedelic hippies as primitive Christians recalling our generation to ultimate values; yet the hippies do in fact sense the bankruptcy of modern values, sometimes more than do churchgoers. American hippies, Dutch *provos*, and their like know that life within the shallow materialistic humanism of our age is meaningless, and in radical protest they are repudiating it, science and all. Whether by LSD, sexual license, or something else, they are probing for a wider, larger world.

Great masses of people, convinced that reality cannot be reduced to abstract mechanical formulas, are skirting the scientific quantification of life in other ways. While radio astronomers are trying to decipher the program of an evolving cosmos, multitudes read the daily horoscopes. Spiritism is at home even in sophisticated centers. The story of Bishop James Pike is well known. Librarians in many American cities report growing interest in books on extrasensory perception and also in the so-called "kook" stuff, literature about flying saucers and the mysterious fringe that baffles even the scientists.

A second development in modern life poses perhaps an even greater barrier to Christian commitment. The present generation has latched onto a new ideal labeled "the good life," and it is the subconscious source for some of the reluctance to entertain an evangelical commitment. Professor Donald MacKinnon, of Corpus Christi College, Cambridge, thinks that "the most deep-seated unwillingness to take seriously the claims of the Christian religion may have its root" in our time not in "the unintelligibility and inadmissibility of such fundamental concepts as that of a creator God, and immaterial soul, etc.," but rather, "in a sharp criticism of Christian ethics, of the Christian image of the good life."[1] Nietzsche thought the Christian attitude toward suffering repulsive and a sign of weakness. Some moderns think the Christian ideal of the good life seriously hinders "men and women from securing and even enjoying the richness of experience which the future may even now furnish themselves and their descendants."[2]

Most of the world's population today is under twenty. Born in an age of mass media and space travel and likely to live into the twenty-first century, this generation is in love with life, eager to explore other planets, and destined to outstrip its predecessors on every hand. It will scarcely rally to a religion that wraps life in parochial don'ts. It needs to be shown the cosmic Christ, to hear of God's great purpose for the whole of creation, to learn of Christ's redemptive work that points to a new heaven and earth. As never before, this is a day for proclaiming a comprehensive Christian world view. We must match today's spirit of cosmic adventure with a dynamic Christian challenge to discover and fulfill God's great purpose for both all the universe and human history.

In an era of man-made satellites and moon walks, what feeling of expectancy, what measure of world mission, what sense of cosmic destiny does evangelical Christianity display? When the whole younger generation senses with awe that we stand within the borders of the space age, what exhilaration, what challenge to unprecedented cosmic adventure, do we communicate?

The anticipation is growing today that "the future" holds a higher, better hope for mankind. Anyone still able to learn from history will sense the futility of simply trying to "escape forward." It is man himself, not the rules of life's game, that needs to be changed. The new ideal of "the good life" encompasses attitudes toward life, toward sex, for example, that make some of our traditional religious proscriptions look very strange indeed.

Yet surely fullness of life and an infinity of sex are not synonymous; in a carnal age that makes sexuality life's foremost concern, the reminder has its point. As the British commentator Malcolm Muggeridge remarks, "Anyone who suggests that . . . the contemporary cult of eroticism, underpinned by the birth pill, and fortified by the greatest outpouring of pornography yet known, runs directly counter to the Christian way of life, is sure to be condemned as a lifehater."[3] That in heaven there will be no giving in marriage may even rob heaven of much of its appeal for those who would least of all forego the pleasures of sex.

But there is another side to the coin. Religious traditions sometimes are just that and little more—traditions of the elders rather than declarations of a sure Word of God. Today's youth will not let even the pope of Rome drape the nimbus of infallibility around what it suspects to be mere tradition. And we shall not gain a hearing for sound biblical perspectives by simply repeating Victorian clichés in the name of the law of God and the gospel of Christ. Jesus warned the Pharisees that tradition can make the Word of God void. What does the Word of God say? That is the decisive issue. Against its clear declarations our own pronouncements and the contemporary mood must be judged. Whether we herald its claims will be the determinant of whether Evangelicalism will possess a breadth of Christian truth to match and surpass the modern vision of life.

If evangelical Christianity offers a richness of life not for sale in the Secular City, if it heralds a hope that can warm the coldest heart, if it guarantees a future that can surpass the prospect of a sojourn on the moon, if it can open the modern soul once again to the transcendent world, if its revelation of God can demonstrate the power and joy of new life in the spirit, then now—*now*—is the time to trumpet the good news.

4

Christian Theology in a Runaway World

NO ONE ALIVE to the intellectual ferment of today's world can escape considering the ever expanding problems new medical knowledge, for example, or nuclear fission or the specter of famine create for the age-old issues of human birth, survival and death. Are we to go on stockpiling nuclear weapons? Should we collectively limit the world population, and if so, by what criteria? When does a fetus become a human being? *Who* is the self that has not merely artificial limbs, but another person's heart, a twin brother's kidneys, plastic intestines, and a cadaver's eyes? Is a doctor duty bound to save life in all circumstances—in cases of deformity and abnormality, of chronic pain, of senility? Is a physician morally obligated to keep alive a body that has sustained irreparable brain damage? Or has he a moral obligation to destroy it? One could go on; such moral problems cry for attention and will not be stilled.

In the 1967 Reith Lectures, published as *A Runaway World?*, Dr. Edmund Leach addresses the problems and calls on scientists themselves to play the role of God and recreate the universe on bold new lines.[1] In place of historic Christian theism he advocates a revolutionary scientism. Dr. Leach, an evolutionary humanist, envisions a new heavens and earth latent in modern science.

Let me offer two preliminary comments. The first bears on the context in which Dr. Leach sets the problems; the second,

25

on his proposed manner of solving them. The Cambridge anthropologist tells us, in effect, that God was never alive, that Christianity is dead, and that Jesus Christ can be wholly ignored. In his view, truth and the good are highly flexible notions. In fact, as Dr. Leach sees it, all morality is "specified by culture" and arbitrary.[2] If there is any universal morality, he tells us, it "gets no farther" than that no society "has yet" been found in which a man may properly have sex relations with his mother.[3] Dr. Leach insists that a changing world involves a changing morality and excludes permanent, universal ethical principles.[4]

Before my second preliminary comment, let me outline briefly Dr. Leach's plea that scientists replace God (or the myth of God, on his premises). Science has, in fact, already become nature's creator, he argues, inasmuch as it has power to redesign the face of the earth and to decide which species shall survive. A number of statements in the Reith Lectures and his short essay "When Scientists Play the Role of God" in the London *Times* emphasize scientists' godlikeness.[5]

He says, for example, "The ordinary everyday achievements of science, which we take quite for granted, are of precisely the kind that our medieval forbears considered to be supernatural." Men now fly through the air, see events on the other side of the globe, transplant organs from corpses to living bodies, change one element into another, and "even produce a chemical mimicry of living tissue itself." "The scientist can now play God in his role as wonder-worker."[6]

"Modern medicine has given the doctor almost unbelievable powers to preserve alive creatures that nature would previously have destroyed, power to change the life prospects in the womb, to alter the personality of the living, and to extend the life span of the senile."[7] "Because God traditionally had unlimited power to intervene and alter the natural course of events, it made sense to treat Him as the ultimate moral authority as well. . . . But today when the molecular biologists are rapidly unraveling the genetic chemistry of all living things—while the radio astronomers are deciphering the program of an evolving cosmos—all the marvels of creation are seen to be mechanisms rather than mysteries. . . . In the resulting mechanistic universe all that remains of the divine will is the moral consciousness of man himself."[8]

Notice now the next step in Dr. Leach's argument. God, he says, traditionally had moral sovereignty because He had "supernatural powers of creation and destruction," but today scientists have these very powers. This new potentiality must be guided by moral judgments, and for these, continues Dr. Leach, "there can be no source but the scientist himself." "It is no good for the scientist to suppose that . . . some outside authority . . . can decide whether his experiments are legitimate or illegitimate. . . . The scientist must become the source of his own morality." And "so we must now learn to play God in a moral as well as in a creative way."[9] Scientists, in other words, are omnicompetent to chart the future of our planet and to decide what is morally right and wrong.

This brings me to my second comment. The emergence of scientists who profess competence in themselves to create, destroy, and impose moral preferences poses a serious threat to human dignity. This arrogance is a threat to civilization itself and must be unmasked before it is too late. Neither the twentieth nor any other century can permit Dr. Leach or any other scientist to play God.

Let me cite Dr. Leach to illustrate why this is so. When medical science was underdeveloped, he points out, "The traditional theological principle that it is always virtuous to save a life . . . made perfect sense." But today, when doctors can preserve deformed infants and senile invalids, the financial burden to the normal and healthy will "at some point . . .

become intolerable, and saving life will become morally evil."*

Now, let me quickly agree that the medical profession and you and I all face urgent ethical problems stemming from the vastly increased capabilities of medical science. But it seems to me that connecting the morality of preserving a life with financial feasibility helps the problem very little; in some countries medical costs now run so high that it is cheaper to let many normal, let alone other, patients die. But let us overlook this; in formulating the issue Dr. Leach could have done better than to suspend ethics upon economics.

Far more important is the fact that Dr. Leach wants to elevate the scientific community as moral arbiter and thinks the scientist is justified under some circumstances in forfeiting rather than saving human life. Since he disowns permanently valid moral distinctions and regards ethical judgments as simply a cultural reflex, may not his future Science City sooner or later welcome the destruction of various classes of human beings? To say that medical science has progressed to the point where it can distinguish between human beings worthy and unworthy of preservation, opens up, in the absence of objective moral principles, an ingenious range of possibilities. A merely culture-bound morality could assert no fixed principles that guarantee to any human being exemption from scientific liquidation.

Let me be fair to Dr. Leach. He deplores the Nazi scientists who experimented with Jews as if they were animals, and he considers Hitler's gas-chamber atrocities to be criminal.[10] The Nazi experiments were predicated on the assumption of the Aryan, so-called higher, race, in respect to which

---

*This statement in Dr. Leach's essay in *The Times* goes significantly beyond the view expressed in his earlier Reith Lectures, where we read: "It would surely be odd if . . . our Christian morality should lead us to avoid having children so as to have sufficient resources to preserve the lives of the maimed, and the senile, and the half-witted? It is hard to say such things, and I repeat: I myself have no solution. But it seems to me that at some point we may need a new religious attitude" (*A Runaway World?* p. 61). /This new "religious attitude," that is, that "saving life will become morally evil," he rests in the *Times* essay on economic considerations.

the Jews were considered undesirable, or virtually "not really human beings at all."[11] In distinguishing humans from nature, Nazi scientists "merely drew their line in a different place," that is, dealt with Jews as if they were a part of nature only, and not really human.

Dr. Leach, in fact, pleads the cause not only of persecuted Jewry, but even of "our subhuman neighbors" such as plants and insects, insisting that "the good and the bad, the weak and the strong, all have a right to exist."[12] This is indeed a curious turn, since the scientist in playing God may distinguish between human beings worthy and unworthy of life, and that not on the basis of absolute moral principles but in view of contingencies. Subhuman plants and insects, however weak, he grants a right to exist, while human beings are presumed at some stage to forfeit their right to existence.

Moreover, Dr. Leach thinks it would be criminal to dissect living human bodies for the advancement of medicine.[13] But if senile persons are actually no longer human, as Dr. Leach's thinking suggests, might not a culture-bound morality consider it more desirable to perpetuate the scientific utility of the senile than to let them die? Or might a pragmatic, unprincipled scientist-god perhaps play it both ways?

Dr. Leach may find what I am now about to say about the latent ethical monstrosities in his thinking to be fanciful and even reprehensible. But let me say it, nonetheless. His culture-bound morality fuses a specious ideology with a high prospect for intolerance. As he sees it, evolutionary progress depends upon abandoning Christian theism and belief in supernatural moral commands; the Christian belief in God and the good must be discredited so that scientism can arbitrate the destiny of man and the world. If this is so, I should like to ask, will not those who hold a supernatural faith be considered retrogressive? Because of their retarding effect on "progress," would they not ideally be eliminated? What further evidence does Dr. Leach need of intellectual senility than that some men repeat the Apostles' Creed and actually believe in God and in the resurrection of Jesus Christ?

Were Dr. Leach a prototype of God, kindlier strands in humanism would likely prevent moral relativity from expressing itself in anti-Christian practice as well as anti-Christian theory. But such deterrents are not inherent in a relativistic view of morals; they spring, at their deepest level, from a biblical understanding of life and gradually disappear with its rejection. While Dr. Leach considers the Nazi pogroms dastardly, Nazi scientists themselves acted on his very premise that no outside authority can decide whether experiments are legitimate or illegitimate and that man himself must be "the source of his own morality." Only the lingering remnants of the biblical perspective can protect a changing morality from thoroughgoing relativism. Dr. Leach's projected labeling of human beings as worthy or unworthy of survival has fearsome implications.

For their spectacular achievements modern scientists merit our full respect and admiration. But to say that the scientist qua scientist is specially gifted to determine all the fortunes of the human species is arrogant presumption. When this scientific pretension spirals into a self-nomination for divinity, we may have the threat of something far worse than Hiroshima or Buchenwald. I, for one, am not ready to let Dr. Leach play God without more persuasive credentials.

Now let me set these comments in the context of the present crisis in theology. Precisely man's frustration in the face of death—which the scientist may delay but cannot overcome—ought to have given Dr. Leach second thoughts about clothing the scientist in the attributes of deity. If anything, man's frustration in the face of death gives the figure of Jesus Christ more rather than less importance for our times. Yet, significantly, the Reith lecturer leaps over Christianity without a single reference to divine revelation or to Christ's resurrection or even to Jesus Christ Himself. Such omissions derive from influential liberal speculators who have tried for decades to make Christian theism more palatable to modern biases, but who in their compromises have succeeded only in accelerating the capitulation to radical scientism. What makes speaking of false gods possible today is yesteryear's theological eclipse of Christ's resurrection and theological silencing of the self-revealing God. For a century and a half modern theology has confronted the age of science with only shadow ghosts of the God of the Bible. Idealistic and humanistic replacements of the "benevolent personal deity called God by a benevolent impersonal deity called Evolution" presaged still other substitutions, some with only a half-day popularity.

That Bishop Robinson's God-is-love-everywhere thesis fails to impinge at all on *A Runaway World?* is a case in point. "Love and do as you please" was supposed to accredit Christianity to a scientific age, but Dr. Leach's projection of tomorrow's world does not mention love even once as a significant value. God is dead, and His cremation included the values peculiarly associated with Jesus. The American radical theologian Paul van Buren would salvage those values after scuttling the supernatural in deference to scientific method. For Dr. Leach, both the Christian God and Christian values must be disowned; Jesus is not mentioned at all, and "the Holy Family" appears only as a misleading image of ideal family life. Just when the God-is-dead theology has exhausted itself in America, the motif is being revived in Britain in order to enthrone the frontier scientist as god.

How could Christian theology of the recent past accommodate and even, indirectly, stimulate this trend toward irreligion in the world of learning?

For one thing, academic studies of science, of ethics, and of theology have each been conducted separately. This separation has been blessed by modern scholars in all three disciplines, but it has been modern culture's loss. Evangelical theology insists the Christian world view has implications for every aspect of human thought and action; sealing off the problems of life in unrelated compartments inevitably distorts their discussion. If for long decades the scientist has neglected to consider the implications of ethics for his work, with what propriety can he, when suddenly faced by life-and-death concerns, assume moral leadership? Does he but legislate his own preferences on the specious ground that all morality is arbitrary? Does might make right and the scientific superman reincarnate Nietzsche's *Ubermensch?*

The twentieth century's greatest need is to recover an understanding of the all-pervasive part played by the divine Logos in human thought and existence. The Logos of God is the agent in creation, in redemption, in sanctification, and in judgment; Dr. Leach can in no way change that. What he has done is to attest the costliness of the Logos' absence in contemporary culture as the unifying principle of religion, philosophy, ethics and science—indeed, of all reality and experience.

The New Testament relates logic and reason to their metaphysical ground; it recognizes the Logos to be the foundation of rationality, of order, and ultimately of the unity of truth. No less a scholar than Alfred North Whitehead acknowledged that Christianity's faith in the sovereign Logos was an indispensable element in the rise of Western science. Christianity supplies an incentive for seeking a coherent understanding of the world and life.

"Part of the trouble," Dr. Leach remarks, "is that we still take our cues from the first chapter of the Book of Genesis."[14] Actually, the biblical narrative of man's creation and fall puts the gloating arrogance of revolutionary scientism in proper spiritual perspective. Replacing divine moral commands with personal or cultural preference (cf. Gen 3:5) is a move not toward utopia but toward calamity.

The story of Adam sets the creativity of man, that is, his mandate to subdue the earth, in the context of the Creator's spiritual and moral purposes. Man was made to have dominion under God and to live in the service of his fellowmen. Not the scientist as God, but all mankind under God, can lift the fallen creation to its ideal destiny.

Because it lost hold on the truth of revelation, modern theology was unable to challenge the new god-pretenders and was, in fact, busy fashioning minigods of its own. Dangled on the leash of modern philosophy, Christian theism lost intellectual power and force. Whereas the collapse of philosophical rationalism might have signaled a new opportunity for the religion of revelation, the positivist rejection of speculative metaphysics brought with it the repudiation of Christian theism also.

Three times in the twentieth century the dominating formulations of Christian theology have crumbled. Each of the influential theories—liberalism, dialectical theology, and existentialism—exploited certain facets of the biblical tradition while rejecting the remainder; each in turn collapsed through neglect of important elements of the Judeo-Christian revelation. Even a quick look at these neo-Protestant compromises shows why scholars were tempted to conclude that God is dead, that revelation does not tell the truth, or that theology is meaningless nonsense.

If Dr. Leach mistakenly thinks the idea of God is a product of history, a number of modernist theologians supplied him with ample precedent. If he asserts that religious beliefs rest not on reason but solely on faith, dialectical and existential theology promulgate this distortion of Christian commitment. If he speaks of God in terms of "Christian mythology," he merely reflects existentialism's mislabeling of the supernatural as myth. If he thinks the throne of deity is vacant, he has allies in recent God-is-dead propagandists who also vaunt scientific method as the only jetstream into the future.

Twentieth-century Christianity has, therefore, little reason to point with scorn at present-day scientific candidates for deity. It ought, rather, to weep for a world church that no longer agrees on God's existence or definition. It ought to weep for a church that transforms theology from the science of God into a rationalization of divergent falsehoods about Him and dignifies the result as devout witness.

One governing bias seems to run through the past fifty years of nonevangelical Protestant theology, namely, the denial that man has rational knowledge of God. Even theologians who contend for divine revelation join those who reject it in stripping all assertions about God of cognitive finality. Ritschlian modernists, Barthian neosupernaturalists, and Bultmannian existentialists— despite all their emphasis on divine revelation—in principle agree with logical positivists that no universally valid knowledge of God is possible. No objective revelation of God, they say, can be found in nature and history. The reality of God is solely an experience of personal decision.

Although each has different reasons, the logical positivist school and the dialectical-existential school agree that no assertions philosophers and theologians may make about God are to be honored as universally valid truth. Metaphysical statements cannot declare what actually is the case. The logical positivists repudiate metaphysical statements on the ground that such assertions are unverifiable by the methods of empirical science. Tested by their (continually revised) verifiability principle, assertions about God were made to appear as meaningless nonsense. The existential and dialectical theologians hold that God reveals Himself personally but not propositionally. They castigate metaphysical predications about God as speculative vanity, and emphasize, instead, the personal demand of the living God for faith and obedience.

The Bible, of course, is brimming with the living God's demands for obedience, but it is also replete with propositional assertions and metaphysical affirmations about God, made on the basis of God's self-revelation. It tells who and what the Deity is and what He does. While neither the Old nor the

New Testament contains a formal, systematic definition of God, the very heart would be cut out of the Bible if its assertions about the living God were to be removed. Above all, the Bible witnesses to the fact that the living God steps out of His hiddenness to disclose Himself and His purposes, intelligibly and identifiably, to man as a rational-moral agent. Anyone who ignores this fundamental feature of the Bible makes a mockery of any further appeal to it.

The tragedy of philosophy and theology's long detour into metaphysical negation is fourfold. First, it drove deeper the wedge between belief and knowledge, between faith and truth, in ecumenical expositions of Christianity. Second, it created a climate congenial to the death-of-God mirage and encouraged religious skepticism. Third, it largely abandoned objective metaphysics to the neo-Thomists and the Marxists. Fourth and worst of all, it showed that evangelical Christianity's academic influence, despite its popular appeal and evangelistic vitality, had so waned that its counterprotest counted for little more than a "we told you so."

Another neo-Protestant option is now entering the vacuum in metaphysics with a bold bid for attention. Metaphysically affirmative, it considers itself superior to evangelical theism as a modern framework for expounding the Christian religion. This option is process-metaphysics, built on the philosophy of Alfred North Whitehead, who distinguished himself both at Cambridge and Harvard universities in the early decades of our century. Currently being refurbished in a variety of ways, process theology is now being aggressively championed by such American liberal theologians as Bernard Meland, John Cobb, Jr., Schubert Ogden, and Donald Day Williams. At Cambridge it is being energetically expounded by Norman Pittenger and Peter Hamilton. All have recently written books supporting process theology and criticizing traditional Christian theism.

Process theology, in brief, denies that God is sovereign, supernatural, timeless, unchanging deity; it makes the uni-

verse as necessary to God's perfection and being as it makes
God necessary to the being and perfection of the universe.
Instead of "a benevolent impersonal deity called Evolution,"
it offers, with somewhat more sophistication, a benevolent
personal evolution called creative becoming. It is, however,
no more likely to impress the modern scientific mind adrift
from Christian moorings than the other modern minigods.
Nonetheless, it will doubtless gain theological attention and
visibility from ecumenical trend-samplers. While it is metaphysically affirmative, it ensnares reason in the evolutionary
process, and it loses the divine Logos' intelligible self-revelation. It claims to give a logically coherent exposition of the
nature and activity of God, yet it disavows any valid or final
assertions about superempirical entities. It is therefore but
another chapter in the neo-Protestant revolt against the God
who reveals Himself intelligibly.

The crisis in theology has its roots in the modern revolt
against divine authority and revelation. Scientists can scarcely be blamed one-sidedly for the revolt so long as neo-
Protestant theologians continue to set the pace.

Only by reopening his spirit to the divine Logos can modern man recover the reality of revelation and the scope of
reason, and regain his lost sense of human dignity. That
Jesus Christ mediates the reality and knowledge and grace
of God and that He sets men free from sin's power and the
grip of death is the central affirmation of the Christian gospel.
In considering issues raised by the Reith Lectures, issues such
as the identity of God, the predicament of man, and the
problems of life and death, the significance of this affirmation
should not be overlooked. The Logos of God, and the Logos
alone, can illuminate the haunting questions of our age with
the light of the eternal world.

5

The Future of Religion

WITHIN SIGHT of the year 2000, today's scientists seem surer of what religion is than do the theologians; many theologians, on the other hand, seem surer of a firm future than do the scientists. From scientists more than theologians come apocalyptic warnings that humanity's survival beyond the twentieth century is doubtful; if nuclear weapons do not get us, air and water pollution will. Our doom may already be sealed; our poisoning of the environment may already have exceeded technology's ability to reverse. Meanwhile, theologians leapfrog over their unresolved differences concerning the past and their existential frustration with the present in order to floodlight the future with a theology of hope.

Scientists, moreover, seem sure that religion is a definable entity, some specific, identifiable facet of human history or experience. Theologians, by contrast, remain remarkably disagreed over what religion is. Many neo-Protestant theologians readily regard atheism as a religion, some deny that biblical Christianity is a religion, and others insist that anything can be a religion if it is taken seriously enough.

The multiformity of religion is, of course, everywhere apparent. The great religions of the modern world, spiritism in Latin America, Billy Graham's spectacular crusades, drug hallucination, and ecumenical social activism mirror its diversity only in part. In the opening chapter of his epistle to the Romans, the apostle Paul focused on the wide and contradictory range of religious practice in his day, and in earlier,

Old Testament times, religious pluralism was of frequent concern to the prophets.

Modern scholars have long sought a denominator common to all religions and religious experience. On remarkably diverse presuppositions, such as pantheism, atheism, and theistic evolution, they have sought to exhibit a distinguishable, definitive, and universally applicable meaning of the term *religion*. But whether they survey the many external varieties of religion or analyze subjective psychological experiences held to be religious, their characterizations turn out to be highly indecisive. The distinction of religion from nonreligion and of religious from nonreligious behavior seems invariably to rest upon special presuppositions or personal preferences introduced by the interpreter. The search for religion's identifying features has failed; religion shows itself to be a phenomenon so complex as to be incapable of definition.

Gordon H. Clark's insistence that "religion cannot be defined" is wholly convincing.[1] The varieties of dogma, ritual, and emotional response associated with religion are too diverse. L. W. Grensted said candidly, "The definition of religion is impossible. . . . The only means of saying what we mean by religion must be empirical, descriptive, and accumulative."[2]

The differences between concepts held by different religions are often obscured semantically; terms like *God* do not mean the same thing in different religions, and acting as though they do only engenders confusion. But different religious thinkers define the idea of God so diversely—as a supernatural Person, as an impersonal cosmic force, as humanity itself, as Father Divine, and so on—that even the devil would qualify did the uninhibited modern mind consider belief in Satan still valuable. Gordon Clark is quite right: "When a term like God is stretched to include every first principle that anybody has ever thought of, and every fetish, spirit and superstition . . . the term means nothing.

. . . Most words in the dictionary have three, four, or even five somewhat different meanings; but if any word had a thousand meanings . . . nobody could tell what it meant."[3]

Not even belief in God is necessary to religion. Hinayana Buddhism, recent American humanism, and Communism, which, although the sworn enemy of religion, is widely recognized as having the features of a religion, are evidence of this. The growing tendency to regard as religious whatever evokes a feeling of the sacred, impels one to ultimate decision, or "turns one on," has so widened the amorphous connotation of religion that one need not hesitate to identify the contemporary youth rebellion as a religious phenomenon of the first magnitude. Paul Tillich regarded ultimate concern as the very essence of religious experience, and whatever concerns man ultimately he held to be religion. Consequently, the whole cultural enterprise may be seen as a religious phenomenon, and atheism becomes an impossibility, even if God's death should be incontestable.

The two most significant religious developments in the twentieth century have been the collapse of ecumenical Christianity into a theologically incoherent movement of arrested missionary vigor and the emergence of atheism globally as a mass phenomenon.

At the beginning of this century the World Student Christian Movement mobilized many hundreds of university students to win the world for Christ in a single generation, and thus carried forward the dramatic Christian missionary expansion of the previous decades. Not long thereafter the rising ecumenical movement marshaled the institutional energies of long-divided denominations for merger into a single world church. But by the late 1960s ecumenical enthusiasm was clearly on the wane; neo-Protestant ecumenism had replaced the historic theological convictions of the Christian church with sociopolitical priorities and had forfeited much of the evangelistic and missionary momentum of the mainline churches. Moreover, as financial support lagged, conciliar ecumenism began living on capital reserves. Church growth, evangelistic vigor, and stewardship gains survived mainly in the so-called third-force and independent churches. Most university students opted out of the established churches. Few were vitally interested in ecumenical merger, and many seemed unsure that institutional Christianity deserved to survive. Meanwhile, non-Christian world religions experienced something of a resurgence; some even penetrated the western hemisphere with a deliberate missionary intention to respiritualize the West's secularized culture.

Today's escalation of atheism is a new phenomenon in human history; the unbelief of an isolated cadre of lonely intellectuals has now become a mass movement of formidable proportions officially supported by powerful modern nations. In Russia and other Eastern European countries once highly sympathetic to the Christian religion, atheistic Communism is now politically entrenched. Official rulings and propaganda are hostile to supernatural religion and severely restrict it. The subjection of mainland China by an atheistic regime has eroded traditional Confucianist ethics and has oriented life mainly to material concerns in an Asian country whose 825 million inhabitants represent almost one-quarter of the population of our planet.

The important atheistic influences in the Western world have by no means been solely Communistic. There is religious humanism; initially the view of disillusioned Protestant modernists, it gave the idea of God only functional rather than ontological significance. There is logical positivism; it boldly limited cognitive knowledge to empirically verifiable propositions and dismissed God-talk as meaningless nonsense. There is theological existentialism; by correlating faith with the nonobjectivity and nonexistence of God, it put personal decision in a cognitive vacuum. It obscured rather than enlivened the reality of God and moved toward existential atheism.

However one assesses the present religious scene, it is obvious that Western despiritualization and the spread of atheism, on the one hand, and the theological imprecision, credal ambiguity, and missionary deceleration of ecumenical Christianity, on the other, are developments of the first magnitude.

Judging simply by population trends, it is quite unlikely that Christianity will claim more than 25 percent of the world's people by the year 2000, over against its present 30 percent. But the determinative issue is not a matter of birth statistics. Rather, the deliberate forfeiture of the convictions that shaped Christianity and the redemptive mission whereby it became the Western world's inherited religion is what spells continuing decline for Christianity. Without a recovery of the spiritual convictions and vitality which marked the church as she came into existence, Christianity is unlikely to remain a serious contender long among world religions. Only a decisive reversal of the neo-Protestant trend can remove the sting of Jesus' question about His own followers: "When the Son of man cometh," He asked, "shall he find faith on the earth?" (Lk 18:8). The contemporary pattern implies a decreased commitment by a diminishing minority to the original distinctives of the Christian movement.

If the number of persons now exposed to totalitarian atheist rule far exceeds the 825 million inhabitants of mainland China, another 825 million persons are virtually cut off from Christianity in the "silent world" of illiteracy. No less astonishing is the church's failure effectively to challenge the mass media, to which vast multitudes have constant access, to reexamine their concentration on material values. Nor has the church effectively utilized the mass media to widen interest in the eternal world. The Protestant Reformers hailed the printing press as a providential gift for the distribution of the Bible to the masses; ecumenical Christianity has not made correspondingly effective evangelistic use of radio or television. Rather, it has used these media to debate the relevance of Christianity itself and its task in the modern world. That the mass media should become prime means for obscuring the claims of Judeo-Christian religion is ironical, for, among the great religions of the world, the God of the Bible is incomparably the God who speaks and shows Himself. He is the God who confronts man audibly in His Word and visibly in Jesus Christ.

Among the controlling beliefs on which biblical religion rests are (1) that the God of Abraham, Isaac, and Jacob has specially and intelligibly revealed Himself as the sovereign Creator of all life and the Redeemer of men to whom He shows mercy, and (2) that Jesus Christ, who was crucified, is alive as the divine Saviour of sinners and the coming Judge of all mankind. Without these convictions the New Testament would not have been written and the Christian church would not have come into being.

The apostle Paul, who was deputized by the Sanhedrin to persecute the early Christians, identifies these assertions, "that Christ died for our sins according to the scriptures; and that he was buried, and that he rose again the third day according to the scriptures: and that he was seen" (1 Co 15:3-5), as the message preached in the first churches. This message he himself came to accept and to proclaim.

But precisely these—the cognitive content of divine revelation, the historicity of Christ's resurrection, and its eschatological significance—neo-Protestant theology has obscured. Only in this last half of the twentieth century is theological discussion being forced to recognize that the faith of Moses and Paul was not asserted in a cognitive vacuum and that the bodily resurrection of Jesus Christ is the cornerstone of the Christian community.

Such observations in a lecture on the future of religion may seem, perhaps, a preoccupation with historic Christianity. But two facts should be borne in mind. However obscure religion in general may be, historic Christianity can be clearly defined. And the question of Jesus' resurrection has important philosophical overtones.

Religion in general is a nebulous concept; historic Christianity can, for some men, be made altogether too clear. Moreover, its claim to special divine revelation, if authentic, gives to historic Christianity a permanent and incomparable role in the world of religion. Christianity explains the universality of religion by the fact that God is real and has revealed Himself; the multiformity of religion it explains by man's sinfulness. For it, the plurality of religions is not an evolutionary development from some common religious essence; rather, the diversity of religions is due to a sinful devolution, through demonic influences, of God's universal revelation of Himself.

While Karl Barth was wrong in contending that biblical Christianity is not a religion, he was surely right in insisting that the God of the Bible discloses Himself in a special way and that this redemptive revelation sets the God of Abraham, Isaac, and Jacob apart from all the speculative deities of religion and philosophy. Those who contend that revelation is common to all religions simply dilute the term beyond recognition. Among the world's living religions a God who speaks is found only in Judaism, Christianity and Islam.

Moreover, if Jesus Christ is risen from the dead, He is in truth the Messiah of Old Testament prophecy, and Muhammad has gone far beyond the truth and is a false prophet. Now, as always, the question of truth in religion is solely a question about the truthfulness of the Bible's claim that it alone offers the one true religion.

Today a growing interest in Jesus' resurrection from the dead is apparent. The question has important philosophical implications. Whenever Western man has cherished a hope of immortality apart from trust in Jesus Christ as the crucified and risen Saviour, he has based the belief on the idealistic or pantheistic notion that some aspect of the human *psyche* is essentially divine and hence immortal. In the pre-Christian world this view was developed by Plato and the Stoics. In modern times, Hegel was its special champion.

Throughout the centuries this speculative belief in immortality has had to cope with doubts concerning the certainty of individual personal survival within an ongoing divine Mind or Spirit. But the twentieth century has vacated that nagging subquestion by shattering confidence in the essential divinity of the human spirit. The tenets of Freud and the deeds of Hitler must surely call in question a doctrine of human immortality based upon the inherent divinity of man. Observation and experience rather supply ample reason for meditating on the biblical teaching: "There is none righteous, no, not one. . . . All have sinned, and come short of the glory of God" (Ro 3:10-23). For Western man the idealistic-pantheistic rationale for immortality has lost credibility. If no other hope exists for life after death, then each day simply brings man that much closer to the grave, and human existence depreciates daily in significance.

Full-hearted commitment to Christianity and credence in Christ's bodily resurrection are not restricted to backward minds. We moderns too often forget that Paul, the great apostle to the Gentiles, was a gifted Jew whose intellectual career included study in the university city of Tarsus and service in the Sanhedrin. We forget that Luke, who wrote the third gospel and the book of Acts, was an erudite medical doctor. We forget that the leaders of the Protestant Reformation were all university-trained men. We forget that, as I mentioned before, at the beginning of our century hundreds of university students went to the ends of the earth to win people of all lands and races to the gospel of Jesus Christ.

At Oxford and Cambridge universities today hundreds of students gather voluntarily on weekends to examine the claims of Christianity; on a Saturday night at Oxford I addressed 325 students on the subject of divine revelation. In our own country not a few college and university students have surged ahead of their professors in probing the Christian faith. Indeed, they often criticize the institutional church and academia as well for failure to present the religion of the Bible and the claims of Jesus Christ on their own historic merit. They decry, also, the peremptory way in which Christianity is often presented only in terms of the short-lived presumptions of modernism, humanism, neoorthodoxy and existentialism. Many alert students refuse to equate the disappearing deities of recent philosophy and theology with the living and eternal God and Father of Jesus Christ.

It is an indictment of Pontius Pilate that he never waited for an answer to his own question: "What is truth?" It is even more incriminating that so few modern theologians hold the question of valid religious truth to be of abiding concern and that so many in pursuing experience and psychic phenomena have stumbled past the historical revelation of the risen Christ.

Today half the world's population is twenty years of age and under. Among the most restless of this throng are the 20 million college and university students, almost half of them in the United States, who crowd the campuses of the world. On these campuses are almost all the future leaders in science, politics, education, literature, the arts, philosophy and religion. In Communist lands, dialectical materialism is ingrained as the only authentic world view, and only those students who disavow the church receive posts of leadership and influence. In the Western world, student thought is hard pressed by a pluralistic approach to truth and values, a philosophy equally incompatible with the Christian revelation. Both atheism and relativism in the academy are inimical to biblical religion.

Religion nonetheless has an assured and prolific future. Not even Communism has been able to daunt or destroy it in Eastern Europe. It has, in fact, had to adopt a more concessive attitude toward religion. But even if Communism drove Christianity and other supernatural faiths underground all around the world, such suppression would scarcely be the end of religion; it would be but to make a global religion of Communism and forcibly substitute one highly arbitrary metaphysical view for others.

I thoroughly disagree with those who have opted for scientism or secularism and expect technological civilization to eliminate the religious dimensions of human life. It is true, of course, that the Christian faith with its belief in the sovereign Creator dedivinized the cosmos. In denying they were gods to be worshiped, Christianity freed nature and civil government for the introduction of natural and political science in the service of man under God. This does not mean, however, that Christianity must now be transmuted into a secular theology that seals off the supernatural, or that science and politics are no longer answerable to the holy Lord of the universe. To think that the God of Christianity can be completely assimilated to the world process, or to identify the kingdom of God with the changing politico-economic possibilities of human history, is to misunderstand what Christianity is.

What then can be said about the social significance of religion in the years ahead? Surely in the future religion's impact on the masses will be minimal unless it speaks as much to the problems of society as it does to the problems of the individual; modern science and politics will quickly disadvantage religions whose only concern is with man's internal spiritual needs. In view of their common claim to be life-giving and life-enhancing, the influential world religions can be expected to speak to social concerns more extensively than they have.

It should be recognized that Christianity has some clear advantages in the whole area of cultural dialogue. For one thing, it has already passed through the Western scientific revolution. Moreover, the call for social justice is not alien or irrelevant to the religion of the Bible, but actually finds its source and sanction there. No civilization has long flaunted the Ten Commandments and survived, and no life has ever rivaled Jesus of Nazareth in holy love. At no time anywhere has anyone called for a more thoroughgoing transformation of man and society than have the biblical prophets and apostles, who demanded not only environmental change, but also and basically individual regeneration. The Christian world view envisions redemption and renewal of the whole of human life and culture; God calls even the most radical revolutionaries to repentance and new life.

For all that, Judaism and Islam have leveled some disconcerting complaints against Christianity. Despite its social activism, Christianity has failed to shape a cohesive religious community in which private and public concerns, especially affairs of state and culture, are meaningfully coordinated. Neo-Protestants concentrated on political involvement in secular society; in doing so, however, they neglected the church itself as the new community that displays the kingdom of God. On the other side, those who held most strongly to historic biblical beliefs tended to concentrate their public energies on evangelism. That evangelism is integral to historic Christianity goes without saying. But only the articulation and putting into practice of a comprehensive, distinctively Christian world view will demonstrate that Christianity is not a pauper in the marketplace of ideas.

When all is said, it remains clear that the vision of a new society is essentially biblical; the demands for social justice have their roots in the prophetic religion of the Bible. The vision of social justice is a Messianic vision. To the extent that Communism protests social injustice and calls for social justice, it is itself an indirect product, however distorted and truncated, of Christianity. But when Marxism puts the state in the place of God as the source, stipulator, and sanction of human rights and duties, it destroys the very possibility of social justice. It no longer has a basis for any ethical norm.

Considering the illimitable spiritual resources of biblical

religion, contemporary Christianity has been shamefully in-
effective in countering Communism. Churchmen frequently
dignify Communism as a Christian heresy, when in fact there
is nothing Christian about it. It is openly and officially anti-
supernaturalistic. Christian moralists have naïvely equated
socialism with the ethics of Jesus and have represented Jesus
as a revolutionary. In keeping with Marx, they often depict
the forced changing of social structures as the main task of
the church.

No wonder the impression gets around that Christianity, no
less than Communism, expects the final fulfillment of human
aspirations within history itself and primarily as a by-product
of socioeconomic changes, independent of modern man's personal commitment to Jesus Christ. In this framework Christian activism is welcome for the support it gives to secular
social causes. The slogan "God speaks in revolution" gathers
much of its momentum from the covert premise that the God
who in the past spoke to Christians through Christ and the
Bible must now become vocal on the side of radicals and
extremists or be considered a victim of laryngitis.

While Christianity has an outspoken interest in social
ethics, its presuppositions are hardly to be found in the
phrase "immanentizing the eschaton," that is, confusing
heaven with the 1980s. Nor does Christianity designate impersonal social structures rather than persons as the basic
candidates for conversion or obscure the universal significance of Jesus Christ as Saviour and Lord. The convictions
of Christianity are quite to the contrary at each point, and by
trumpeting them, evangelical Christianity can become a
formidable alternative to both neo-Protestant ecumenism and
atheistic Communism. But it must coordinate its scattered
energies into a vast transdenominational, transracial, transcultural thrust that encompasses Christian involvement from
evangelism through education to social concerns.

Religion cannot fail to survive, and Jesus Christ cannot fail
to judge it; but whether evangelical Christianity survives in

the next generation depends on the course it chooses in the present. Unless another Great Awakening sweeps them, the evangelical churches may find themselves groveling on the sidelines of modern history.

6

What I Think of the Ecumenical Movement

TWENTIETH-CENTURY CHRISTIANITY is currently torn between
two ridiculous extremes. Unless the Christian church rises
above them, the cause of Christ may waste away in these
next years like the proverbial donkey starving of indecision
between two stacks of hay. Here I discuss the folly of independency and the foible of ecumenism, and then conclude
with some remarks on the future of Christianity.

THE FOLLY OF INDEPENDENCY

By the folly of independency I mean the almost endless
proliferation of denominations and, beyond that, the eager
readiness of isolated groups of believers to seal themselves
off from almost everything and everybody else. I am not
denying that many persons in such communities may belong
to Jesus Christ; our Lord Himself promised that where two
or three gather in His name, He will be in the midst of them.
Nor do I accept the monolithic propaganda that denominations are inherently sinful. But if Israel could get along with
twelve tribes, perhaps the church, too, could manage with
no more than a dozen denominations.

I am weary with the folly of independency. In my college
days I became a Baptist as a matter of personal conviction,
and I still think Baptist roots strike very deep into the sub-
soil of the New Testament. But there are so many varieties
of Baptists today that even Luther Burbank would have des-
paired. A young Anglican assistant curate, left to serve alone
in his parish during summer holidays, was asked by a Baptist

family newly moved into the area to take a funeral service. The vicar was gone, the curate was gone, so the young assistant cabled his bishop: "May I bury a Baptist?" The answer came back: "Bury all the Baptists you can!" There must, I think, be some happier way out of our dilemma.

Let me offer five observations on independency:

1. It is impossible for believers to opt out of the body of Christ. We need one another for well-being and survival, not simply for amusement and diversion. A body without some of its vital members is in need of a skin graft or a heart transplant or some other radical surgery. I am not saying simply that all Baptists need all Baptists; rather, I am saying that all Christians need all Christians. No variety of Baptists—nor any other denomination—is self-sufficient. The day has dawned in church history when all Christians not only need one another, but also need to thank God for one another and to find one another.

2. The church of Jesus Christ is a commmunity, not a clique. Most unfortunately, the sense of being a family, of being a new community of redeemed persons, has gone out of many of our churches. Persons who commit themselves to Jesus Christ often become very lonely people. Former associations no longer do; old relationships give way. Often new converts come into our churches bearing all sorts of burdens. Are they welcomed as into a new family? Or are they unsure they can entrust themselves and their problems to others? Are newcomers uncertain whether they will be understood?

The many breakdowns, spiritual and mental, in our churches are a double tragedy. Individuals venturing into a new way of life honoring to Jesus Christ and facing complex new problems are often left to carry their burdens in secret and to fight their warfare alone. No human companion shares the load or points the way. This tragedy can happen as readily in a church of a hundred members as in a church of a thousand. Yet the church of Jesus Christ ought to be a family with fellowship so warm and intimate that people outside will secretly long to be invited in. Does the spirit of independency run so deep in our church life that we isolate ourselves not only from believers in other denominations, but also from believers in our very own churches? What has happened to the church as *koinonia*, as a family fellowship?

3. Jesus Christ alone is Head of the church. He has no favored puppets, any more than He has a first lieutenant in Rome, and Jesus Christ assesses the Christian community with scrupulous honesty. He still walks among the churches, threatening to remove lamps from their candlesticks. If He can endure the compromises of modern American Christianity no more than those of ancient Asia Minor, all these lights we consider so indispensable could suddenly be blown out.

It is a tragedy of independency that miniature popes arise here and there who make the agencies and organizations of others a target of unfair propaganda; they promote their own causes and raise funds by demeaning what others are doing in Christ's name. They even distort the truth, and such distortion seems to increase when the closer—and therefore more competitive—the ideals and goals of the agencies they aim at are to their own. Independency too often means the legitimation of private prejudices and the sanctification of religious orneriness.

Jesus Christ alone is Head of the church, and I have yet to be persuaded that He has opened a branch office in Rome, or Geneva, or Collingswood, New Jersey, or Wheaton, Illinois, or Valley Forge, Pennsylvania, or on New York's Riverside Drive.

4. By failing to transcend their isolation and independency, evangelical Christians have virtually forfeited a golden opportunity to shape the religious outlook of the twentieth century. For twelve years as founding editor of *Christianity Today* I pleaded with evangelical Protestants to venture beyond independency into interdependency in common witness. The interdependency we need involves a mutual de-

pendence on Jesus Christ as Head of the church. I stand by the convictions I expressed in 1967 in my *Evangelicals at the Brink of Crisis* that the decade ending in 1975 will see the curtain lowered on the evangelical movement as an important religious force in contemporary American life unless its independency and isolation are transcended. The World Council of Churches knows better than to concentrate its energy mainly on criticism of others' programs. It is time for evangelical Christians to learn that ball games are not won by a multitude of individualists booing the batters, but by a team running bases and scoring points.

What I have in mind is not simply organizational merger between, for example, the National Association of Evangelicals and American Council of Christian Churches (although there are no heavenly reasons—only earthly excuses—why believers in these movements ought not to be united). I am not really talking about merger at all; merger ought to come spontaneously at the climax of a romance, not by the fiat of ecclesiastical elders at its beginning. And surely I don't wish to imply that the NAE and ACCC encompass anywhere near to all the significant evangelical forces in American Protestantism. More American Evangelicals are outside than inside these movements. Many are hidden in the National Council of Churches, and many are not affiliated with any cooperative agency. But by their separateness the NAE and ACCC publish the scandal of evangelical division.

No Christians have insisted more than we that Christian unity depends upon doctrinal agreement. But while no other major Protestant group has more theological consensus than does American Evangelicalism, nowhere on earth is there a group of Christians more divided.

I have serious reservations about the adequacy of institutional merger as an answer to the problem of the disunity of Christians in the modern world. At the same time, I am not convinced that adding more rings to the evangelical circus, however glamorous the riders, is in the interests of biblical

Christianity. Year after year, decade after decade, the evangelical witness has reflected a crippled and disjointed strategy, precisely when all its forces needed to be rallied for con-
certed witness. Evangelicals desperately need to overcome
their isolation and disunity.

Dr. Paul Rees, former editor of *World Vision* magazine,
tells of a remarkable incident in the days of his Minneapolis
ministry. In a rural town in northern Minnesota a man needed
a surgical operation that no local doctor could perform. The
patient was driven to Minneapolis in an old hearse that was
doubling for an ambulance. The trip was rather tedious, and
it happened that just as the ambulance got into heavy downtown traffic the patient raised the window curtains to see
where he was. Terrified pedestrians rushed into the path of
the hearse and shouted in desperation, "Driver, your corpse
is alive!" The tragedy of many evangelical Protestants today
is that they think they are running an ambulance when the
world sees only a hearse. Unless we find new union in Christ,
the world may overtake us in astonishment to cry out, "Christians, your body is a corpse!"

The Foible of Ecumenicity

The ecumenical vision is a dream that may turn into a
mirage. Anyone who thinks the organizational combina-
tions of the past generation have brought in the kingdom of
God or fulfilled Jesus' high-priestly prayer for the unity of all
believers lives on an ecumenical cuckoo cloud. The foible of
ecumenicity lies in the notion that church renewal can be
achieved by blending separate denominations into a larger
mixture that perpetuates all the ailments and afflictions of the
component parts.

1. It is one thing for denominations to reshuffle ecclesiastical furniture; it is another for believers worldwide to mani-
fest their unity in Christ. The great denominations today are
coordinating their power structures. That is hardly identical
with oneness in Christ.

Union with Christ is the fundamental union that Christianity is to promote, and yielding priority to any other kind of "joinery"—whether joining a world organization, joining a denomination, or joining a program—is a costly error. The difference between a body and a corpse lies not in the organization of the material elements, but in the spirit which supplies its life. One does not produce a live body by joining together two corpses.

2. Today criticism of institutional Christianity is a flood at its crest, and the ecumenical movement now stands as a major specimen of institutional religion. Another massive religious institution is the last thing in the world a Muslim, Hindu, or Buddhist needs to be converted to. There is less enthusiasm today for one great world church than there was ten years ago. Some communions are more interested than ever in a world federation of their own denominational churches, for example, the Lutheran World Federation; others show increasing interest in national federations of churches.

The defeat of Anglican-Methodist union in England is a sign of the times; had it succeeded, there would have been three denominations—two of them protest denominations—instead of the original two. The Baptist Union of Great Britain and Ireland reported earlier this year that 168 churches favor continuing with the World Council and British Council of Churches, that 323 churches have no clear view in the matter, that 164 churches favor withdrawal, and that 1,559 churches did not even bother to reply to an inquiry.

Much that preoccupies the clergy today in the way of ecumenical merging is taking place wide of the hearts of the laity. Many laymen couldn't care less about the merging of denominational institutions. A leading Anglican layman active in the world of business investment, when reading details of the Anglican-Methodist merger proposal, remarked: "I don't know much about theology, but I recognize a phony prospectus when I see one." A growing number of laymen now think that the church of Jesus Christ is sitting loose of the institutional church and that private homes may again become the front door to the church.

3. At the same time, beneath the surface the institutional church is becoming polarized in many ways. The conflict between institutional and noninstitutional perspectives is not simply an ecumenical-versus-evangelical difference. The institutional church is now being challenged from within by "young Turks" who concentrate on a radical politico-economic message, and by Evangelicals on the inside who want evangelism given priority.

The debate over the church's role in social action continues; some Evangelicals still overreact to the liberal "Social Gospel" by confining the Christian message to personal experience, and some liberal churchmen mistake every move by conservatives toward social involvement as a tardy endorsement of their social gospel. The phrase "Christian action in society" now means so many different things that it is a cliché.

Some observers think that the church in the near future will take very different forms, novel and unpredictable forms. In some lands, staggering cultural upheavals beset the churches. In totalitarian lands they are driven underground; in lands of resurgent non-Christian religions, Sunday has become a workday, and believers must gather for worship before and after they go to their jobs. But also arising are distortions and caricatures of the church, satanic distortions that recall some of the New Testament passages about the blasphemous monstrosities of the end time.

On the other hand, some observers think that when present trends come fully to the surface, there may be an immense cleavage in the church commensurate with the Protestant Reformation and even surpassing it. From the church in the home, from a renewal of the laity, from new evangelical outcroppings will come a realignment of believers. The conviction will coalesce among Christians that the largest issue is not the question of organizational affiliation or nonaffiliation, but rather the question of evangelical fidelity or infidelity.

THE FUTURE OF CHRISTIANITY

When I speak of the future of Christianity, I have in view especially evangelical Christianity. Without an authentic experience of Jesus Christ, the Christian community does not have a ghost of a chance of making a distinctive impact upon the world; further, it has no distinctive impact to make. The early Christians had a clear message and a transforming experience; their preaching centered on God's deliverance which they had made their very own.

1. The evangelical vanguard can afford to be preoccupied by one burden only, that of standing shoulder to shoulder and heart to heart in radiating to the world Christ's deliverance and the blessings of serving the one true God. It must not be mesmerized by hallowed traditions; it must not be spent in shoring up sacrosanct ecclesiastical structures; it must not be diverted by newer demands for organization.

2. Evangelicals cannot afford to make organizations the prime target of their propaganda, pro or con; nor can they afford to make the issue of organizational identification or nonidentification the determinant of evangelical authenticity. Some people try to make a gospel out of ecumenism or antiecumenism, and such a gospel can only be a false one. Evangelical Christians must keep the truth of revelation as the subject and center of propaganda; fidelity to God's Word and union with Christ must be their test of fellowship.

3. If I have three basic criticisms of contemporary Christianity, they are these: First, that ecumenical Christianity neglects the truth of revelation and advances its cause through theological imprecision. The inevitable result is that the message of the church shades off into ambiguity. Second, that evangelical Christianity, for all its biblical vitality, does not shape communities of redeemed persons that stand out in the world markedly visible for the quality of their fellowship.

Finally, that evangelical Christianity does not propel into the world an evangelical vanguard that claims the entire world of work and education and culture for Jesus Christ. Let me add a brief word about each.

First, without the truth of the gospel, without worship of God in spirit and in truth, the church may as well close shop. All the activism in the world cannot compensate for a loss of the truth of revelation. Christians belong in the vanguard of the drive for social justice, but to march to the tune of secular revolutionaries is actually to be in the "tailguard." Ecumenical Christianity sorely needs to recover the revelation of God and the authority of the Bible. It is sheer irony that Roman Catholic observers often bring Protestant discussions in the Central Committee of the World Council of Churches back to a theological and spiritual basis.

Second, without a demonstration to the world of the fellowship that the gospel nurtures among redeemed persons, without a manifestation of the kingdom of God in miniature, the church of Christ cannot hope to make effective headway in the modern world. Make no mistake about it: to proclaim the gospel is not simply to say the right thing in the right way at the right time; it is also to do the right thing in the right way at all times. The message of Christ needs to be embodied no less than to be verbalized.

It will take more than people commuting to and from church buildings, more than boldness in witnessing verbally to others, more than theological fidelity, to shake the modern world into an awareness of the reality of God. For multitudes the church seems now to be antilife; society is elaborating its own version of the "good life," one that deliberately incorporates much that has long been "off limits" for human dignity and decency.

How can the Christian community confront this generation with the fact that all the best things to which a man can aspire are promised in the kingdom of God? It cannot hope to do so if the church rolls are mainly a roster of unregenerate members; you can't find new life among people who are not reborn. It cannot hope to do so if Christians exhaust their time and themselves fighting each other. Nor can it hope to do so if the church exhausts herself in institutional mechanics. The church must be a mirror of the kingdom of God to the world. If she is not, why should her message be heard?

Finally, the evangelical community must provide leadership in the whole social order. It must pervade the world of work, the arena of education, and the whole range of cultural life with creative service to God and neighbor, devotion to the whole body of truth, and dedication of all one's gifts to the nobler impulses of life. It must point man to a fuller and finer investment of his energy and hold before him the vision of a world in which the joy of the Lord is restored to the ways of men.

7

Christ and the Crisis of Our Age

IN THE WEST TODAY book title after book title contains the word *crisis*. The revolt sparked by the French Revolution against all the structures of the past and against every claim of the supernatural world has gained swift momentum. No generation has thrown more scientific light on man and the universe than ours; but in moral and spiritual matters, today's world gropes in drear darkness. Contemporary civilization is in retrograde decline, like an unsure missile tumbling and yawing in space.

This crisis is spiritual. Modern man is estranged from God, the infinite Spirit who alone can properly be worshiped "in spirit and in truth." In some great universities today it is said that talk about God signifies nothing intelligible.

This crisis is moral. Modern man plays leapfrog with God's commandments and presumes to relativize the standards by which He will judge men and nations.

This crisis is intellectual. Modern man not only acts counter to the truth, but, even worse, he does not seek the truth. And he rationalizes his revolt against the truth of God by saying that all assertions about the real nature of things are subject to revision.

This crisis is social. Modern man does not love his neighbor as himself. He does not love as he ought, nor does he serve justice in public affairs, though he makes clichés of scriptural ideals such as neighbor love and justice. Where is there today a nation on the face of the earth in which God delights? Where is there a society with the stamp of the Holy Spirit upon its ways and works?

This crisis, in short, touches the whole of humanity and the whole man. The soul of modern man has been sucked dry by temporary concerns that eclipse the eternal world. Family life and marriage, the domain of work, and the political world are in turmoil. The distinguished psychologist Rollo May observed that in the mid-twentieth century the chief problem of people is "emptiness."[1] Man, who was made in the divine image, lives virtually in the image of the apes and seeks to compensate for his hollowness by sensual satisfactions. The man of the West, who has 3,000 years of philosophy, the comforts of modern technology, and revealed religion as part of his inheritance, seeks fullness of life through an infinity of sex, things, and status. The man of the East, standing amid ancient religions, likewise finds life a vacuum that neither the traditions of the past nor the novelties of the present can fill. The twentieth-century world has a gaping hole in its heart, and it is gradually dying from the lack of whatever makes life truly life.

Look magazine carried a comment made to Bishop James A. Pike by his twenty-year-old son just a few months before the lad committed suicide.[2] Gone was his father's liberal optimism about man and society; gone was the confidence that social action can shape a brave new world. "The way I got it figured is this: You might as well live now. There's sure as hell nuthin' to look forward to in the future. I say, play it cool—stay uninvolved. Take what you can get when you can get it and forget it, man. That's the only way to live."

Not many weeks later word came to the stunned bishop in a church service: "Your son is dead; he shot himself." "Live now . . . live fast . . . that's the only way to live." It was "life" without a future, the "good" without a future, "the only way to live." It all proved to be not really life. It was mere temporary endurance that contained, as young Pike himself put it, "sure as hell nuthin' to look forward to in the future."

Never since biblical times was the bent of a generation more exposed than ours by the declaration of Jesus Christ: "Search the scriptures . . . they are they which testify of me. And ye will not come to me, that ye might have life" (Jn 5:39-40).

Notice that "Christ and the Crisis of Our Age" connects Christ and our crisis by the conjunction "and." Nobody realized better than our Lord Himself the necessary connection between His historical appearance and the destiny of humanity. He wept over Jerusalem, not simply because of the stony hardness of men's hearts, but also because His own ministry of grace had made men's final decision unavoidable and unpostponable. Jerusalem and all Jewry could not turn back the clock of world history or of saving history—not even for an hour, not for a moment. The time for ultimate decision was *now*.

It was true that God had sent His Son into the world not to condemn the world but "that the world through him might be saved," that "God so loved the world, that he gave his only begotten Son, that whosoever believeth in him should not perish, but have everlasting life." But no less true was it that "he that believeth not is condemned . . . because he hath not believed in . . . the only begotten Son of God" (Jn 3:16-18). "Now is the *crisis*," said Jesus; "now is the judgment of this world" (Jn 12:31, free trans.).

So, too, the apostle Paul gave notice to the Gentile world that the time of its ignorance was past. Not only has the day of judgment been appointed, but by His resurrection God publicly identified the coming Judge. The resurrection of Jesus points to man's inescapable future; the time for repentance and human decision is *now*.

Alongside the empty, hollow and inauthentic life of modern man stands the offer of life that is truly life. "Fullness" describes the life of Christ in the gospels, and in the epistles "fullness" in the Holy Spirit becomes a badge of authentic Christian existence. To live a life that is not filled with the

Spirit is to live a life that is beneath the dignity of a Christian.

Evangelicals will fail this generation if, in speaking as witnesses to the redemption that is in Christ Jesus, they distort or dilute the fullness of the evangelical message. Christendom today shows scars almost everywhere from speculative distortion and experiential dilution of the message of the Bible. If Evangelicals cry out in indignation against the modernist and the existentialist perversions of revealed religion, they had best prepare themselves also to cry out in repentance over their own subevangelical presentation of it.

It is not too difficult to answer the question: "What is an Evangelical?" An Evangelical is a bearer of the evangel, the good news, that Jesus Christ died for our sins, that He was buried, and rose again the third day, and that all this took place in accord with the inspired writings (1 Co 15:1-4). An Evangelical is one whose outlook is biblically validated and who recognizes in Jesus Christ, the incarnate Logos, the crucified and risen Redeemer promised in the Old Testament. An Evangelical will not need to mumble phrases of the Apostles' Creed, for he knows God, the Creator, Redeemer, and Judge, who has revealed Himself in Scripture and in the person of Jesus Christ.

It is more difficult to answer the question: "Who is an Evangelical?" Not everyone who says, "Lord, Lord" will enter Christ's kingdom. Presumably not everyone who professes to be an Evangelical will, either, even if he qualifies the terminology and says, "Dear Lord, dear Lord." An Evangelical, I said, is a *bearer* of the evangel, and I take it that means in his person, and not simply on his lips.

How did the early Christians win their way in the first centuries of our era? The Stoics had frozen human emotions to the point of resignation. The Epicureans had shriveled moral horizons to "eat, drink, and be merry, for tomorrow we die." The collapse of classic philosophy had left the intellectuals in chaos. Those Christians knew the truth of revealed religion, indeed, but they knew the truth both in propositions and in their own persons. The truths they knew were life-transforming. They knew the Holy Spirit, who fills and refills and fulfills life, so that now they hungered and thirsted for righteousness. Even Christians unskilled in philosophy could meet a great mind like Augustine, and that brilliant pagan would be attracted to them because of the spontaneous joy that infused their lives. This hints that even the pagan secretly knows that truth and joy must somehow belong together.

Christian slaves lifted human dignity, and they became the carriers of the moral fortunes of a pagan empire. And among pagans who exposed their relatives to die, Christians ministered compassionately to the dying; and self-serving unbelievers were constrained to exclaim, "See how they love . . . !"

And why did they love with a love that evoked that "how"? They loved because God had first loved them in their unworthiness; because God *so* loved. They knew that to withhold love from other human beings on whatever pretense—inferior social standing, color, race, creed, or whatever else—would have been to deny in principle the love that God had shown in Christ. Christ had died for them when they were worthy only of condemnation and death. They loved, and even pagans secretly sensed that self-giving love and the truth of God must go together.

The early Christians had the spontaneity and reality of the Christian life "going for them" and running apologetic "interference" for them even before they started talking about the hope within them. They knew the incredible love of God, who rescued them when they had forfeited all right to rescue. They knew the risen one, who in His victory over death somehow included them. They witnessed to others, not simply because Jesus Christ had commanded them to—although indeed He had. They witnessed because they had new life and new hope, and because they wanted men everywhere to meet the coming King.

In the global crisis of our time—perhaps the consummating crisis of all time—if evangelical faith is to command attention, it needs courageous young men and young women as leaders. The cause of the gospel today needs disciples young enough to run to the tomb and to soar over the seas and to leap into space with good tidings. Never did men need more to know that *the* crisis of our age is—as it has been for every age—the matter of decision for or against Christ.

8

Christ Appeared!

IN THE MAGNIFICENT CHAPTER 15 of 1 Corinthians the apostle Paul interprets the meaning of Jesus Christ's resurrection. Since the importance of our Lord's resurrection or nonresurrection can hardly be overstated, I consider the consequence, the coherence, and the character of Christ's resurrection, looking especially at verses 1 through 11.

THE CONSEQUENCE OF CHRIST'S RESURRECTION

1. Does the Christian church rise from a mirage, and does the New Testament rest on a myth? Or is the only convincing explanation for the birth of the Christian church and the origin of the New Testament the fact that after His death the crucified Jesus Christ showed Himself to be alive again?

2. Is the resurrection a dispensable doctrine without which the Christian religion would be spared a great deal of embarrassment? Or would losing the reality of the resurrection jeopardize the whole structure of Christian belief? According to the apostle Paul, the resurrection of Jesus Christ is not simply one link in the chain of Christian doctrine; it is a historical event basic to Christian faith without which authentic hope collapses.

3. Is bodily resurrection an utterly incredible notion, the least believable of the options available to modern man, or is it the only credible option that remains to us for life after death? Modern psychology regards man as a unity of mind and body, as a psychosomatic whole. Man's final destiny, whether mortality or immortality, seems therefore to involve

his total self, and not just the doom or survival of a fragment of the self.

4. Did the early Christians actually find new life through the risen Christ, or were they, in accepting the accounts of the resurrection, victims of a colossal deception? Were they actually united to the risen Christ as the glorified Head of a body of redeemed and regenerate believers, or was their Christian fellowship a fantastic illusion?

In short, on the resurrection of Jesus Christ depends the legitimacy of the Christian church, the trustworthiness of the New Testament, the validity of Christian doctrine, the plausibility of the life to come, and the authenticity of Christian experience. Consider, therefore, the coherence Christ's resurrection has in Paul's account.

THE COHERENCE OF CHRIST'S RESURRECTION

On the likely assumption that it was written in the early '50s and before any of the gospels, 1 Corinthians would be our oldest literary testimony to the resurrection. In it the apostle Paul carries us back to sources that antedate not only his writings, but also his own conversion. In 15:3-5 (ASV) he repeats a formula which apparently was in use in the primitive Christian churches even earlier than Paul's conversion: "For I delivered unto you first of all," he writes, "that which also I received: that Christ died for our sins according to the scriptures; and that he was buried; and that he hath been raised on the third day according to the scriptures; and that he appeared to Cephas; then to the twelve." The earliest churches presumably used this summary in proclaiming the gospel or in catechizing converts.

But Paul does not stop with the earliest Christian preaching; he goes back even farther to eyewitness reports of what happened on resurrection weekend.

He does not stop even there. Jesus' resurrection was no bizarre contingency that defied human logic. It was not an utterly incoherent incursion into history. However unique and unparalleled as a historic event, the resurrection of Jesus Christ took place in a coherent framework of meaning. Its context stretched back far beyond the events of Passion Week.

1. Divine revelation had prepared orthodox Jews to believe in the resurrection of the dead. The Pharisees believed in a universal resurrection at the consummation of history (cf. Ac 23:8). The sister of Lazarus shared that expectation: "I know that he shall rise again in the resurrection at the last day" (Jn 11:24).

But the Pharisees believed that in no case would the dead be resurrected before the end time. No doubt they expected that in the distant future Jesus Christ would also be raised and that God would then condemn Him as a false Messiah. The resurrection of Jesus was not for them a logical, historical or scientific impossibility; what they could not accept was that it had already occurred, not at the end time, but on the third day after His crucifixion. What the Pharisees insisted could occur only as the preface to the coming new age, the Christians declared had already taken place: in Jesus Christ, God's new age had drawn near.

2. The context of Christ's resurrection is even wider; Paul emphasizes that it occurred in accord with God's revealed promises. He does not argue from what scientists consider possible on the basis of predictable regularities in nature, or from what historians consider possible on the basis of analogies with their own experience. Rather, he argues from what God has revealed.

No recent theologian has warned more pointedly than Jürgen Moltmann of Tübingen University that the modern emphasis on causal uniformity arbitrarily limits our understanding of nature and history. For modern philosophy, all events occur with absolute causal uniformity grounded either in pantheistic determinism or in naturalistic determinism.

But the Judeo-Christian revelation emphasizes God's purposes and freedom in nature and history. The resurrection of Jesus is not contingent on some special potentiality that science establishes; it is contingent solely on the power and purpose of God. The same God who raised Jesus pledges that His resurrection is the paradigm for a resurrection of all mankind yet to come in which we all—scientists and historians included—are scheduled to participate.

3. The context of Christ's resurrection extends also to God's comprehensive plan for man's redemption. It involves the gift of His Son, the death of the Redeemer, and His resurrection for our justification. "Christ died for our sins according to the scriptures . . . was buried . . . hath been raised on the third day according to the scriptures."

4. Jesus' intimations to His disciples might also be mentioned. At the time, the disciples overlooked His hints, but after Jesus' resurrection His statements came alive for them. These do not appear in Paul's account, for he, of course, did not share with the other apostles in Jesus' earthly ministry.

However unexpected was Christ's resurrection—even His own disciples did not expect it—the event was neither logically nor historically and scientifically impossible. It stands coherently related to the orthodox Jewish belief in resurrection, to God's own promises, and to His comprehensive program of redemption. All this was part of the primitive church's teaching before Paul's conversion.

Yet what Paul *delivered* was more than what he had *received* from Hebrew-Christian sources, however valid. In view of his special mission to the Gentiles, Paul himself was granted to be a witness of the risen Christ. Nothing less than a shattering religious experience can account for the transformation of Paul's spiritual values and life's vocation. Seeing the risen Christ turned him from an active enemy into Christianity's first apostle to the Gentile world. "He appeared," Paul emphasizes, "to Cephas; then to the twelve . . . to James; then to all the apostles; and last of all . . . he appeared to me also" (15:5-8, ASV).

By this turn of the narrative we are swept beyond the coherence of the resurrection to contemplate the character of the resurrection. "He appeared!" "He appeared to Cephas." "He appeared to above five hundred brethren at once." "He appeared to James." "He appeared to me also."

THE CHARACTER OF CHRIST'S RESURRECTION

Some moderns depict Paul's encounter with Christ on the Damascus road as simply an inner experience or vision. It was a voice of revelation or a subjective spiritual crisis, they say, and then they go on to regard this supposedly internal experience as decisive for the nature of all Christ's resurrection appearances. Paul himself claims that Christ's appearance to him was continuous with the appearances to the other apostles. Is the reality of the resurrection therefore to be reduced simply to an inner spiritual experience of the disciples?

To be sure, the risen Christ personally confronts His followers and through the Spirit of God indwells believers. But for 2,000 years the Christian church has believed that Christ's resurrection is not reducible to simply an inner experience and that objective historical factors distinguish it from an intense communion with Jesus that survived His crucifixion. The early Christians asserted the aliveness of Jesus in terms of a space-time resurrection that was objective and external to themselves. In many ways Paul affirms and implies the objective historical character of Jesus' resurrection.

1. Paul does not hold up Christ's appearance to him on the Damascus road as the paradigm for all the other appearances; instead, he recognizes the other appearances have a certain priority. "Last of all," he writes, "he appeared to me also" (15:8, ASV). The appearance to him was "out of due season," or "as to the child untimely born." How can this possibly mean that the manifestation to Paul is to be regarded as the model for Christ's confrontation of believers in every age? Rather, Paul was vouchsafed a unique, authentic resurrection appearance that was distinguished from the others by its

temporal discontinuity; it occurred after the ascension, when the physical appearances had presumably ceased, and before the end-time Parousia, when "every eye shall see him" (Rev 1:7).

2. That the biblical writers date the resurrection after Jesus' burial and not simultaneously with His death indicates they meant bodily resurrection, not merely soul survival. Burial always involves a particular grave or tomb, and the resurrection involved the buried Christ. "Christ died . . . and was buried . . . and . . . hath been raised."

3. For Paul, "the third day" is not simply the first day of Christ's appearances; it is explicitly the day He was "raised." "He hath been raised on the third day according to the scriptures." This third day "rising" cannot be understood in any other way than "raised from the grave."

4. Although Paul concentrates on the appearances to the apostles, and to himself as the apostle to the Gentiles, for good measure he notes Christ's appearance to more than 500 persons on a single occasion. He emphasizes that most of these eyewitnesses were still alive. "He appeared to above five hundred brethren at once, of whom the greater part remain until now" (15:6, ASV). If by "appeared" Paul were speaking only of an inner spiritual confrontation, this reference to 500 believers, in an epistle written some twenty years after Christ's resurrection, would be nonsense. More than 3,000 converts beheld Christ's glory at Pentecost in the sense of an inner spiritual experience, and by A.D. 50 there were many more than 500 people who could tell about personal communion with the risen Lord.

5. Paul shows beyond all equivocation what he means by the resurrection in his defenses before the Sanhedrin and King Agrippa. He meant the same type resurrection the Pharisees believed in and the Sadducees did not. To the Sanhedrin, Paul said: "Brethren, I am a Pharisee, a son of the Pharisees: touching the hope and resurrection of the dead I am called in question" (Ac 23:6, ASV). Likewise, he re-

minded King Agrippa that by religious heritage he was a
Pharisee, adding: "And now I stand here to be judged for the
hope of the promise made of God unto our fathers; unto
which promise our twelve tribes, earnestly serving God day
and night, hope to attain. And concerning this hope I am
accused by the Jews, O king! Why is it judged incredible
with you, if God doth raise the dead?" (Ac 26:6-8, ASV).

6. My final point on the character of the resurrection concerns the empty tomb. Many moderns hold that Paul's silence
about the empty tomb means either that he disowns the tradition or that he is wholly unaware of it. To this it may be
replied that Paul's emphasis on "the third day" agrees with
the emphasis in the gospels on the empty tomb. By placing
Christ's resurrection in objective space-time, Paul clearly
refuses simply to spiritualize the event.

Some critics call the phrase "the third day" a literary de-
vice. They say Paul used the phrase to emphasize that Jesus
was a real historical figure, contrary to Docetic denials of
His humanity. This contention simply will not stand up. In
separating Christ's death and resurrection by three days, so
it is argued, the New Testament writers indicate only that
Jesus was a truly historical person. But this is nonsense. And
it makes nonsense of passages like "Thou wilt not suffer thy
Holy One to see corruption" (Ac 2:31, quoting Ps 16:10),
which not merely asserts humanity, but excludes physical
disintegration.

Also, as archpersecutor of the early Christians, Saul of
Tarsus surely knew that the resurrection message could be
stilled by an exhibition of Jesus' corpse. Yet, as we know, the
Jewish leaders admitted that they did not possess the body,
and none of Christianity's early opponents—Paul included—
was able to produce Christ's remains in order to silence the
preaching of the resurrection.

There is a good reason why the empty tomb was not the
decisive issue for Saul. That he knew nothing about the
empty tomb is highly unlikely; as an official persecutor of the

Christians he probably knew and spread the Sanhedrin's story that the disciples had stolen Jesus' body. In these circumstances, and removed by a period of several years after the crucifixion and burial, what would count decisively with Paul was not the empty tomb, but a direct sight-and-speech confrontation with the risen Christ. While the disciples needed to be convinced that the risen one was the same Jesus with whom they had lived for three years, Saul of Tarsus needed to be convinced that the crucified one, whose death he approved and whose followers he persecuted, was again alive and was indeed the Lord.

The resurrection of Jesus Christ is of towering importance. Confident that the crucified Redeemer showed Himself alive, the Christian church came into being. By the same confidence all who trust in Christ find new life and hope that is forever sure. By the bodily resurrection of Jesus, God has declared that man's afterlife involves his total being, not a mere impalpable continuance. Christ conquered more than death; He conquered sin and death. It is this sinless, deathless future guaranteed by Christ's resurrection toward which God is moving us. Hallelujah! Christ arose!

9

The Risen Christ and Modern Man

GORDON TAYLOR's *Biological Time Bomb* tells what some scientists project for tomorrow: human sperm stored in cold-storage banks, babies conceived by laboratory techniques that dispense with the womb, people produced from body cells rather than germ cells, extra eyes and other organs grown routinely for surgical substitutions, "cloning" or genetic manipulation to produce duplicates of ideal men, indefinite extension of man's life-span through replacement of bodily parts.[1] Some even speak of hope for physical immortality through permanent conquest of disease.

Now, that is a remarkable turn of events. Modern science has long been thought to destroy the credibility of Jesus' resurrection and with it the Christian's hope of a future life. Now, on the basis of their own growing competence, scientists are holding out the possibility of present physical immortality. They have added a third option to Western man's repertoire of hopes for continued existence.

Traditionally the Western world's expectations for life beyond the grave spring from two different sources. The one theory, rooted in Greek and Roman philosophy and revived in modern pantheism, is that the human spirit is essentially divine and hence immortal. Here no permanent value attaches to man's body; no lasting significance is given to man as a total self, as a spiritual and physical unity. Only man's spirit finally survives, absorbed at last into the infinite Spirit, of which our mind is held to be a part. Man's personal immortality is left in doubt. But it has been a long time, at

74

least a couple world wars ago, since anyone has been able to believe the mind or spirit of man is divine. Moreover, the man who survives without his body, survives as something other than man.

The other view is the Christian view, which affirms not only man's personal survival after death, but also the resurrection of the body. The physical resurrection of the crucified Jesus becomes the paradigm for a future resurrection of all mankind. Christianity stresses the redemption of the whole man. It has no interest in salvaging only man's spirit, and it decisively rejects the pantheistic delusion that man's spirit is divine. The Christian view differs from speculative philosophy in a third respect. It preserves moral and spiritual decision as the context of human life both here and hereafter. Alternatives to the Christian view have no driving moral concern.

The philosophic view regards man's soul as inherently immortal and divine apart from the question of personal righteousness. Come what may, man is a part of God. The divine Spirit ultimately enfolds man's spirit—be his name Nero, Hitler, Stalin, or Mao Tse-tung. Man is God in miniature, and sin, repentance and redemption are inconsequential.

Nor has the modern scientific view a moral vision; it is inherently amoral. The effort to prolong bodily life proceeds irrespective of ethical considerations. If the Mafia alone can afford unending life, if only Nazis are to be preserved, if Stalin is the genetic prototype for "clonic" reproduction, so it will be. Science supplies no fixed moral norms.

The alternatives, then, are pantheistic immortality or scientific prolongation without a sharp moral requirement, or bodily resurrection through Jesus Christ with divine judgment or redemption at its center. The philosophic case for immortality is not credible, and nobody believes that science will finally stave off human death. If all the options for immortality have expired, then every day simply brings us nearer the grave, and life diminishes daily in worth.

In the Bible, man in his totality depends upon the special action of the Creator for his existence. Sin has thrust the whole of man into the grip of death, and to the whole man—body and spirit in unity—Jesus offers rescue. Only if the New Testament hope holds firm is there a sure prospect of life beyond the grave.

Modernist theology long assumed that science had ruled out the miracle of Jesus' resurrection. The dogma that nature is a network of unbroken causal uniformity excluded such once-for-all events. But since the turn of the century, scientists have been increasingly reluctant to claim that their theories tell us how nature is really constituted. So often have the so-called "laws of nature" been revised that most scientists now admit that their formulas only tell us "what works," not "how things are." In any event, Christianity does not base its belief in the resurrection merely upon a certain view of causal connections or disconnections in nature; rather, the whole of nature itself is dependent upon God, who sustains it.

Jesus' resurrection took place according to the plan and purpose of God. "Christ died for our sins according to the scriptures, and he rose again the third day according to the scriptures" (1 Co 15:3). In the resurrection of Jesus, God anticipated the conclusion of history; He openly published the outcome of both church history and world history. As the apostle Paul said to the philosophers in Athens, God has "appointed a day, in the which he will judge the world in righteousness by that man whom he hath ordained; whereof he hath given assurance unto all men, in that he hath raised him from the dead" (Ac 17:31).

Consider the first Christians. What can account for the change in them? They were Jews from the workaday world of fishermen and tax gatherers and tentmakers; they became missionaries to the ends of the earth. They fled in fear at the hour of their Leader's crucifixion; yet they became the bold carriers of a new faith to the whole world. The quavering, fearful ones became bold martyrs.

Devout Jews, they tried to remain inside Judaism, but could not. They now looked upon the Old Testament as filled with Messianic prophecies fulfilled in Jesus of Nazareth, and they emerged from the confines of Judaism into what they considered to be the religion of fulfillment. They gathered to worship one whom both the Jewish and Roman authorities thought to be dead, and did so on the first day of the week, not the Sabbath.

They considered themselves entrusted with good news for every last man, woman, and child on earth. They recognized themselves as members of a new social organism, the church. They were convinced that the risen Jesus is the coming King and future Judge of all mankind. They were gripped by the revolutionary idea that the "third race" of the twice-born, to which they now belonged, will inherit the earth as the rescued family of redemption. For this conviction they offered what meager fortune they had and placed their bodies on the line, counting their earthly lives of less value than the eternal life they had found in Christ.

Central to this transformation stands Jesus Christ as one physically alive after His crucifixion. Without the resurrection the Christian church would not have come into being, and the New Testament narratives would not have been written. Every account of the resurrection converges on the point that a large number of Jews—many hundreds of them—saw Jesus alive after His crucifixion. As C. S. Lewis reminds us, "The first fact in the history of Christendom" is the insistent report of a growing number of people that they had seen and conversed with the risen Jesus.[2] They distinguished this confrontation from an inner psychological experience and declared their testimony to be that of eyewitnesses. Also, the apostles, as we know from the criterion used in selecting Matthias to replace Judas (Ac 1:21-22), were companions of Jesus "from the baptism of John" through the resurrection appearances; their role was not that of church administrators, but of witnesses to the fact that the crucified Jesus had arisen from the grave.

The graduate group chairman of the religion department at the University of Pennsylvania thinks that Christ's resurrection cannot be believed because present experience offers no analogy for such a miracle.[3] Presumably, to become credible, any New Testament miracle needs to happen twice: once in the first century and once again in 1972 in the religion department of the University of Pennsylvania. The God of the Bible does not, however, so readily accommodate professorial demands for private miracles. There will indeed be a second resurrection, a resurrection of all men; of that coming resurrection Jesus Christ is pledge.

But the answer to a modern historian's demand for a repetition of the resurrection is a simple one. Whether something actually happened 2,000 years ago does not turn on a philosophical requirement imposed by present experience; nor is it necessary for theologians to be able to point to empty tombs and abandoned crematoriums in Philadelphia. Questions about the past are answered by historical testimony. The trustworthiness of the answers is certified by the character and competence of the eyewitnesses and by the antecedents and consequences of the event. The million copies of *The New English Bible* sold immediately upon its release provide a far surer clue to the fate of the crucified Jesus than does anyone seeking analogies in a modern cemetery.

10

The Disturbing Shadow of the Risen One

IN A TORONTO HOTEL I happened upon a cluster of newspaper reporters. One of them I had gotten to know in Berlin at the World Congress on Evangelism. "What's going on?" I asked. "Come along," he joshed. "We're interviewing John Allegro in Room 1435." Along I went. Allegro had brushed off the Methodist ministry as a calling and had gained fame by writing an exaggerated book about the New Testament's supposed dependence on the Dead Sea Scrolls. At this time he had just completed *The Sacred Mushroom and the Cross,* a book that professes to derive the Christian religion from the fertility cults of the ancient East.

Somehow it all seemed quite strange. Here was a room full of reporters clustering around a lecturer whose book really is but a footnote to the view dominant in university circles today: that Christianity is not a specially revealed religion, that Jesus Christ was not really born of a virgin and did not really rise from the dead, and that we are not really sinners after all. His was just a variant expression of a worn-out story; yet evangelical giants who *are* saying something different go unreported.

Newsmen do not often interview scholars who stand squarely against the tides of modern religious doubt and insist that the contemporary mind lacks sound reasons for its faithlessness, contending that the supports of reason are on the side of Christ and faith. That the press often prefers to seek out scholars who confirm modern prejudices may reflect some secret uneasiness within the citadels of doubt. Is the

79

case against Christ in such desperate straits that it needs all the negative reinforcement it can get? Why else are evangelical challengers of the reigning spirit of unbelief so generally ignored—and that by newsmen who pride themselves on their alertness in reporting the unusual?

How remarkable it is that modern men simply cannot put Jesus of Nazareth wholly out of mind. It is not simply that many people now shorten the five-letter word *Jesus* and the six-letter word *Christ* into readily available four-letter words. Rather, Jesus Christ has a significance so inescapable that men of decency and dignity, though they may stand aloof from the Christian heritage, still have to wrestle with the great issues He poses, dim though their awareness of what He says may be.

For that matter, not all in the world of learning have moved around Him, past Him, and away from Him. Scholars of *Who's Who* stature in many of the world's most prestigious universities consider the bodily resurrection of Jesus to be one of the best-attested events of the historical past.

Across the hall from Allegro's old office at Manchester University, England, is that of F. F. Bruce. A great New Testament scholar, Bruce holds that no events of the classic world are better attested than those to which the gospels give witness. Bruce is certainly not alone in his confidence in the historical resurrection of Jesus Christ. Others that could be mentioned are J. N. D. Anderson, director of the Institute of Advanced Legal Studies at the University of London, C. E. D. Moule of Cambridge, Hans Rohrbach of Mainz (the brilliant mathematician on whom the Nazis relied to break the American code in World War II), G. C. Berkouwer of Amsterdam, and Oscar Cullmann of Basel. In recent years a major theological movement has sprung up in Germany built around the ideas of Jürgen Moltmann and Wolfhart Pannenberg. They hold that in the resurrection of Jesus Christ, God has indicated the direction human history is moving and the kind of humanity He approves.

Were a list to be drawn up of believing scholars in America, it might well begin with Martin Buerger, former dean of the school of advanced studies at the Massachusetts Institute of Technology, and Gordon van Wylen, head of the school of engineering at the University of Michigan.

For men of this rank the question of competent witnesses is critically important. That the New Testament writers repeatedly stress their role as eyewitnesses is not lost on them. Luke uses the term *autoptai,* from which we get our word "autopsy," to emphasize that the disciples were eyewitnesses. The prologue to John's first epistle is replete with the terms "seen," "heard," and "touched."

After some 2,000 years Jesus Christ still leaves His mark upon men, even in their rebellion. We are still secretly embarrassed by the resurrection. For all modern man's break with the supernatural and the eternal world, he seems unable to reconcile himself to any conviction that he is merely a temporal creature whose threescore years and ten are a prelude to mere nothingness. And our deepest longing for personal immortality has a Christian anchorage—Christ's resurrection. It is that ever present, ever embarrassing resurrection which drives us to the point of decision for or against which drives us to the point of decision for or against Christ *and* provides us with our only glimmer of hope for a future life.

After the philosophic hope of the Greeks and Romans for immortality has faded, after the pantheism of Hegel has withered, the resurrection of the crucified Jesus remains the only firm basis for two of man's cardinal concerns—our personal survival of death, and a life fit for eternity. By eternal life the New Testament does not simply mean an endless existence after death; it means life *now* of a new quality, a new character, a new kind, life given from above by the indwelling of the Holy Spirit. Death does not put an end to any man's existence; rather, it puts an end to the opportunity for life sheltered by the grace of God, for a life fit for eternity, for life on speaking terms with God, for life unshadowed by the judgment of God.

We Americans bury our dead, as anthropologists are driven to comment, in a way that gives them a final semblance of being alive. That is not the only indication of our refusal to yield to the final reality of death. We are now reaching for a pseudo-immortality—maybe even a doubling of man's present life-span—through the continual replacement of human organs. Science is being looked upon as the giver of immortality in this body.

This longing for an indefinite extension of life in the body has interesting comparisons and contrasts with the biblical revelation of man's nature and destiny. For the Greeks, man was essentially a mind; the body was a dispensable prison. For modern psychology, man is a "psycho-somatic" entity; you cannot have man without having a body. The Bible, too, deals with man as a unitary whole; it refuses to identify the essential self or ego simply with the mind or spirit, and it refuses to discuss the body as marginal to man's personality.

Those who decline to speak of a survival of essential human personality once the body goes are not wrong, though naturalists draw the wrong conclusion in saying that physical death marks the end of consciousness. Christian revelation points beyond physical death to resurrection life in a body suited for the eternal order. Man is by creation a compound being; sin affects the totality of man, and redemption does too. Redemption and the future life concern both "parts" of man—his soul and body.

On the surface, modern science and the Bible strike similar notes on the incompleteness of men without bodies. On a deeper level their underlying bases for the assertion are completely different. One place this difference shows up is in ethics. Science does not raise questions concerning the goodness or wickedness of the man it helps. The Bible sets human destiny, in this life and in the life to come, in a moral and

spiritual context. Each man's personal relationship to Jesus
Christ is decisive.

Only if the New Testament hope holds firm is there a sure
prospect of personal life beyond the grave. But the New
Testament doctrine of the afterlife does not stand alone; it
is part and parcel of the Christian view of God and man. It
involves a distinctive view of God. It involves a distinctive
view of origins and of the created dignity of man. It involves
a distinctive view of man's moral predicament, his plight as a
sinner in revolt against the holy Lord of the universe. It
involves a distinctive view of redemption, involving God's
self-revelation, the gift of His Son, Christ's atoning death,
and His bodily resurrection. It involves the offer of new life
—a new birth and a new character with a will transformed
and a mind for the things of God.

As for myself, I was no Saul of Tarsus armed with Sanhedrin documents to harass the Christians. I was a newspaper reporter who had read the resurrection narratives
much as Saul heard the same story in the first churches. I
disbelieved the man from yesterday, yet all the time was disturbed by the shadow of Christ's resurrection. Then one day,
ready to receive the gift God offers a repentant sinner, I knew
I dare not be embarrassed by the miracle.

John Updike puts it this way:

> Make no mistake: if He rose at all
> it was as His body.
> if the cell's dissolution did not reverse, the molecules
>   reknit, the amino acids rekindle,
> the Church will fall.

> It was not as the flowers,
> each soft Spring recurrent;
> it was not as His Spirit in the mouths and fuddled
>   eyes of the eleven apostles;
> it was as His flesh: ours.

The same hinged thumbs and toes,
the same valved heart
that—pierced—died, withered, paused, and then
    regathered out of enduring Might
new strength to enclose.

Let us not mock God with metaphor,
analogy, sidestepping, transcendence;
making of the event a parable, a sign painted in the
    faded credulity of earlier ages:
let us walk through the door.

The stone is rolled back, not papier-mâché,
not stone in a story,
but the vast rock of materiality that in the slow
    grinding of time will eclipse for each of us
the wide light of day.

And if we have an angel at the tomb,
make it a real angel,
weighty with Max Planck's quanta, vivid with hair,
    opaque in the dawn light, robed in real linen
spun on a definite loom.

Let us not seek to make it less monstrous,
for our own convenience, our own sense of beauty,
lest, awakened in one unthinkable hour, we are
    embarrassed by the miracle,
and crushed by remonstrance.[1]

11

Sent into the World

"THE LIBERATOR HAS COME!" With these words evangelist Tom Skinner climaxed his reading from Isaiah 61. His audience was 1,000 college students at Urbana '70; the words he had read were the ones Jesus applied to Himself at the outset of His ministry (Is 61:1-2; cf. Lk 4:18-19). "The Spirit of the Lord is upon me," Jesus said. "He has anointed me. . . . He has sent me." I wish to consider Jesus as the Liberator sent by the Father, then ourselves as coliberators sent by the Son.

Jesus' message had a cutting edge, and His contemporaries, whom He openly indicted for their sins, found it easier to reject Him as a pseudo-Messiah and a rival of God than to accept his message. They pitted the Father against the Son; but Jesus held man's honoring of the Father to be inseparably united to his hearing of the Son. Much of John's gospel deals with Jesus' credentials as the sent Son of God. Throughout chapter 5, especially, the term "sent" echoes and reechoes: "He that honoureth not the Son honoureth not the Father which hath sent him" (v. 23); "He that . . . believeth on him that sent me" (v. 24); "the Father which hath sent me" (v. 30); "the . . . works that I do, bear witness . . . that the Father hath sent me" (v. 36); "the Father himself, which hath sent me" (v. 37); "whom he hath sent, him ye believe not" (v. 38).

The emphasis on the sending Father and the sent Son reaches a dramatic climax in 9:7. Here the man blind from birth, a type of those misled all their lives by the religious leaders, is anointed by Jesus and told to "go, wash in the pool

of Siloam, (which is by interpretation, Sent.)" "He went,"
we read, ". . . and washed, and came seeing." This man knew
the Liberator had come.

For Jesus, what did being sent by the Father involve? He
renounced the glory and joys of heaven. By taking on human
nature, He stepped from the holy presence of the Father
into this sinful world. He lived and died among a race unworthy of His love. In order to restore fallen humanity, He
walked in glad obedience to the Father, even unto death.

Listen to His high-priestly prayer: "I have finished the
work which thou gavest me to do. And now, O Father,
glorify thou me with thine own self with the glory which I
had with thee before the world was" (Jn 17:4-5). For us He
was willing to forego the glory that was His from eternity
past.

He also put aside the joys and bliss of heaven. Hebrews
12:2 reminds us: "For the joy that was set before him [he]
endured the cross, despising the shame, and is [now] set
down at the right hand of the throne of God."

Jesus stepped into human history from beyond, for "no
man hath ascended up to heaven, but he that came down
from heaven" (Jn 3:13). Jesus "came down *from heaven*";
that is, He existed eternally as the second Person of the Godhead before His incarnation. But He did not clutch His status
of equality with God as something to be forcibly retained,
"but made himself of no reputation, and took upon him the
form of a servant, and was made in the likeness of men" (Phil
2:5-7). He assumed, or took on, human nature. "In the beginning . . . the Word *was*. . . . And the Word became flesh"
(Jn 1:1, 14, ASV).

It was to men unworthy of His love that Jesus came. On
every hand He met hostility, misunderstanding and faithlessness. I shall never forget one summer years ago when I
worked as an attendant in one of the largest mental hospitals

on Long Island. How strange, how incomprehensible, how exasperatingly irrational was the behavior of those pitiful patients! How must Jesus have felt, what must He have thought, when He in His perfection walked among us? He knew wholly "what was in man" (Jn 2:25): deliberate waywardness and wickedness and hardness of heart. He met the betrayal of a Judas and the denial of a Peter, lethargy in Gethsemane and desertion at the cross. How much madder must the barbarism and lust of our modern world seem to Him!

Though His own people disowned Him, His brethren disbelieved Him, and His disciples failed Him, Jesus obeyed the Father implicitly. When Satan dangled before Him the enticement of world rule, He obeyed the Father. Even through the excruciating distress of the cross, He trusted the Father. At the end He alluded to Psalm 22, which starts, "My God, my God, why hast thou forsaken me?" but continues with the ringing affirmation, "Thou art holy, O thou that inhabitest the praises of Israel" (Ps 22:1, 3). He obeyed the Father until the very shaking of the earth, and the darkening of the sun, and the rending of the veil of the temple, and (hallelujah!) the bursting of the tomb. Because He obeyed, He arose from the grave as the mighty Conquerer of sin and Satan and death.

Man's sickness and suffering, those constant reminders of death's power in and over us, Jesus turned into occasions of triumph. The holy demands of God's law, which expose us to sin and its wages of death, He matched by His sinless life and substitutionary death. In every way He signaled Satan's ultimate powerlessness over all who put their trust in Him; His perfect life, His healing the sick, His raising the dead, His triumph on the cross, and His resurrection victory are guarantees of His own full and final conquest of Satan.

The Liberator, the sent Son of God, has truly come! Hallelujah!

Jesus was sent by His Father. He in turn sent the apostles, and we, also, in our time, are now sent in His name. As spiritual brethren of Jesus Christ and spiritual sons of the apostles, we also are Christ's legates, and the Great Commission contains our official instructions.

"He that believeth on me," said Jesus, "the works that I do shall he do also; and greater works than these shall he do; because I go unto my Father" (Jn 14:12). "And he gave some, apostles; and some, prophets; and some, evangelists; and some, pastors and teachers" (Eph 4:11). "If any man be in Christ, he is a new creature. . . . And all things are of God, who . . . hath given to us the ministry of reconciliation. . . . Now then we are ambassadors for Christ, as though God did beseech you by us: we pray you in Christ's stead, be ye reconciled to God" (2 Co 5:17-20). "For I have given unto them the words which thou gavest me; and they have received them, and have known surely that I came out from thee, and they have believed that thou didst send me. And now I am no more in the world, but these are in the world" (Jn 17:8, 11). "Neither pray I for these alone, but for them also which shall believe on me through their word; that they may all be one; as thou, Father, art in me, and I in thee, that they also may be one in us: that the world may believe that thou hast sent me" (Jn 17:20-21). "As my Father hath sent me, even so send I you. . . . Receive ye the Holy Ghost" (Jn 20:21-22).

What do these momentous passages imply for us? Stationed in a perplexed world and buffeted in the convolutions of a frantic civilization, what are Christians to be and to do?

We shall never understand our role unless we thoroughly understand that apart from what the gospel of Christ offers, this world is utterly, irrevocably and irremediably lost. Neither the United States nor the United Nations, neither the Communists nor the capitalists, neither scientists nor philosophers nor sociologists nor educators nor psychiatrists nor any other creature can offer anything more than a delaying action for doomsday. Christ alone is able to liberate modern man from the grip of sin. However important the political, academic and scientific enterprises may be—and they are important—this planet is hopelessly lost apart from Jesus Christ. These enterprises, in fact, now constitute part of the problem and cannot be the real hope of the world. If we comprehend this, we shall sense the urgency of our mission in the world.

God's strategy for rescuing men in our time is not dependent on ratification by contemporary man. God's plan was not devised by the human ingenuity of Moses or Isaiah or Paul; nor can any modern Evangelical or non-Evangelical arrogantly presume to point the way. Only the gracious revelation of the living God can illumine the road of rescue. The divine plan for human redemption involved a disruption in the life of the very Godhead; the implementation of that redemptive plan involves a division in the body of humanity. Make no mistake about it: God distinguishes between the redeemed and the lost. Not for nothing did the Father send His beloved Son into our fallen world, and not for nothing did the Father and Son together send the Holy Spirit upon a new society of twice-born persons.

We are sent in Christ's name. For that reason an aborted mission now is as unthinkable as would have been Jesus' disobedient rejection of the Father's will. From the standpoint of God's redemptive purpose, for the church to nullify the Great Commission could only result in dire calamity for both world and church. If Christ tarries, the present ecumenical disengagement from foreign missions, easily accommodated by the prevailing mood of universalism, can only be a source of astonishment for future generations of Christians. The gospel of Christ is, as one minister recently put it, "not only portable, but it is exportable." We have been too barracks-bound; we accumulate large building debts and pay massive interest charges, only to see nonevangelical forces take over properties which we have not been fully using at that. Is this perhaps a judgment on our misconception of the church of Christ as essentially a magnificent building? Christians today are more and more prone to support persons and ventures on the go for Christ, rather than buildings and administrators.

We are sent to multitudes that are spiritually dead and to cities crumbling from moral decay. For all its boasting and sampling of culture's delights, our generation is running scared. Many scholars concede that the mythic presuppositions which govern contemporary man are fast losing power; our age is, in fact, on the brink of intellectual exhaustion. Hopelessness permeates much of the Communist and capitalist worlds alike. Scores of young people are opting for pagan philosophies; multitudes whose parents drifted away from God retain no memory whatever of biblical reality.

Books about urban collapse abound. Secular writers speak openly of the need for "saving our cities." By this phrase James A. Michener in The Quality of Life means salvaging American cities that once did, but no longer do, give intellectual and artistic leadership.[1] "The survival of the city," says Michener, "depends upon the control of crime; without this the hopeful developments will come to nothing, and we shall have lost one of the world's finest inventions: the complex city which has represented the best of civilization."

In Newsweek of February 8, 1971, Stewart Alsop talks about "The City Killer," or heroin addiction, in New York. Of the prisoners in the Tombs, Manhattan's twelve-story prison, 70 percent are heroin addicts. Of these, 95 in 100 will predictably go back on heroin when they are released. At $40 to $80 a day, heroin addiction is a habit they can hope to support only by crime. Alsop estimates that in New York City alone there are between 100,000 and 200,000 heroin addicts who "threaten the life of New York as surely as malignant cells threaten the life of a body." And he adds, "The same malignancy threatens, or soon will, all our great cities."

In view of the needy multitudes, what we need is greater awareness of being personally sent. There is but one alternative to our obedient heralding of the evangel, and that is death—ongoing spiritual death for those who have not responded to the gospel, and moral death for cities and nations unleavened by our Christian walk.

Important as it is to go, it is no less important first of all to wait together in prayer for cleansing and filling and enabling by God's Spirit. Apart from spiritual power, scrambling about the globe means little. It was spiritual power that drew multitudes to hear John the Baptist at the Jordan River. It was spiritual power that attracted throngs to Jesus in the mountains or by the seaside. It was spiritual power that brought Paul a hearing even in the Mamertine Prison.

We absolutely do not have adequate resources in ourselves for meeting the problems of worldly multitudes. Indeed, we cannot by ourselves work out even the problems that beset believers. The time has come for Evangelicals to understand afresh what corporate "waiting" can be, and what it can do in the mission of the Christian church. We need to wait upon the Lord together, in groups as well as alone. Jesus spent long nights alone in prayer; He also prayed with His disciples, even with sleepy ones.

Even after forty days of postresurrection instruction Jesus told His disciples not to launch their mission until they were empowered by the Spirit. The New Testament invariably connects God's love for man with the cross of Christ. It also almost everywhere links the gift of the Holy Spirit with the world mission of the church. The Holy Spirit must stand behind and overshadow the work of the church or we are doomed to failure. He has an indispensable role at the inception of the church and at the entrance of every soul into God's kingdom; those not born of the Spirit cannot behold the kingdom of God (Jn 3:5). Those who had not heard there is a Holy Spirit, Paul knew to be still outside the church (Ac 19:3). The Spirit's presence was the guarantee that the new age was under way. In the book of Acts every forward movement of the church grew out of the Holy Spirit's guidance.

To be sure, we read in the Old Testament of God's Spirit dealing with His people. But in the New Testament the life and invisible presence of Jesus of Nazareth stamp the activity of the Holy Spirit, and the filling of the Spirit becomes a distinctively Christian experience. Through the Holy Spirit's filling, Christians display the distinctive characteristics that reflect the Son of God: honest intention, sincere motivation, disarming love, holy joy. The Spirit of Christ gives a freedom and boldness in witnessing that overcome every attempt to frustrate, without being offensively aggressive. Beyond all that, the outpoured Spirit secures believers in an intimate relationship to God wherein they cry, "Abba, Father."

Let it be emphasized again that not until the Holy Spirit was poured out did Jesus release the church to witness. Pentecost was authentic ecumenism; the Spirit gave utterance (Ac 2:4), and the gospel became intelligible to all men in a foreshadowing of centuries of missionary expansion.

The Liberator Himself has come and has returned to the Father, but He has not forsaken the world. We are coliberators with Him, sent in His name; we must be either on our knees before Him or on the move with Him.

12

The World, the Church and the Gospel

OUR GENERATION is playing leapfrog with the gospel, and this game is more hazardous than Russian roulette. Today, as if some silent conspiracy exists between the two, a hostile world and an indifferent church are, by and large, hedging in the gospel and hopping over it. If we are to break the church loose and to free the gospel and revive for this generation the New Testament drama of a compassionate church with a regenerative message, the church must take fresh stock of the world, the gospel, and itself.

Ours is a world of staggering changes in which great nations like Britain topple from world supremacy, sleeping nations like China stir themselves awake, and new nations like Israel rise from the dust of past ages. It is a world in which mighty civilizations fade and new cultures soar to pre-eminence. It is a world in which, almost overnight, the industrial revolution and technological innovation have transformed our way of living and the very face of the earth. It is a world in which man has learned to walk in outer space without cosmic dizziness, halt the advent of human life with a capsule, postpone death by a heart transplant, and commute to the moon. What a magnificently resourceful world this is!

But it is also a runaway world in which totalitarian dictators destroy human dignity and rights openly, while the democracies do the same things in more subtle ways. Ours is a world in which war has not only gone global but has also taken to the heavens, in which man has split the atom and treated populous cities like Hiroshima to cremation. It is a world running from the random past into a computerized future. Restless of restraints and running from God, it is a world on rampage, a world gone radical, rebellious, and renegade, and a world resistant to divine authority.

It is a world whose population increases by 65 million a year, a world in which many now alive are those for whom, as Kafka put it, "the music has broken off at the root of things." It is a world whose population balance is rapidly shifting to Asia, and one-fourth of our globe's inhabitants are now in Communist China.

It is a world which at the beginning of this century called 33 percent of its population Christian, but which at the century's close may claim that less than 22 percent is Christian. It is a world whose diminishing Christian remnant is starkly aware of the spiritual alienation of once friendly world powers like Russia and is reminded anew of past whirlwinds like Islam's conquest of flourishing Christian communities in Asia Minor and North Africa. It is a world for which God has largely gone silent, and in which long-repressed impulses of man's pagan nature are thrusting into view. It is a world whose gods—science and sex and status and stocks— have left life even emptier than it was.

But it is still a redeemable world. Here is a marvel to dwarf all the wonders of modern science: this world is the object of God's love. The great Creator has not forsaken the rebellious creation: with a love measurable only by the superhuman yardstick of the death of His holy Son, He loves it still. Despite its riot and rebellion, it is *this world* that God loves, and to it He addresses His gospel.

What is the gospel? It is God's good news; Mark 1:14 calls it "the gospel of God." It is God's disclosure, not a man-made speculation. The apostle Paul in 1 Corinthians 15 declares "the gospel . . . by which also ye are saved . . . I delivered

unto you first of all that which I also received, how that
Christ died for our sins according to the scriptures; and that
he was buried, and that he rose again the third day according
to the scriptures: and that he was seen of Cephas, then of the
twelve" (vv. 1-5). This formula may have been used by the
very earliest churches to summarize the gospel and to cate-
chize converts. Nowhere does the New Testament yield an
inch to any relativistic reduction of it.

The gospel is good news about what God is like and what
He has done. It is supremely about Christ, who made the
restoration of sinners to fellowship with the living God possible. The gospel is good news about what Jesus did, not
just what He taught. It is the good news that, though we
deserve divine repudiation and punishment, God offers the
guiltiest of us sinners forgiveness for Christ's sake. That is
the unchanging gospel, and a Christianity that dilutes this
content is not worth its weight in words.

The revealed gospel is regenerative. God's incarnate Son
gave His life for the rescue and renewal of doomed men. To
the Galatians, Paul stressed that Jesus Christ "gave himself
for our sins, that he might deliver us out of this present evil
age" (Gal 1:4, ASV margin). The gospel of God offers rebellious man the only means of restoration to sonship in God's
kingdom; the benefits of Christ's atonement include the forgiveness of sins, new birth, and new life in Christ. The gospel
is not merely a matter of saying the right words in the right
way in the right place at the right time. The legacy of biblical religion includes the indispensable divine gift of a new
heart: "Except a man be born again, he cannot see the kingdom of God. Ye must be born again" (Jn 3:3, 7). New birth
is absolutely essential; without it there can be no new life.

Because the trials and terrors of modern life are heavy and
the world's darkness is deepening, special urgency attaches to
the Christian mission. The gospel alone offers the healing
power all men now so desperately need. Driving in Great
Britain, I was surprised suddenly by a warning sign: DAN-

GER OF SUBSIDENCE. That means "beware of cave-in";
the bottom may drop out unpredictably! The modern outlook is vulnerable to such collapse; it cannot bear the weight
of modern living. We need desperately to recover some of
the long-lost initiative in evangelism. Secularists have held
evangelical Christians at bay too long. How refreshing to
sense the momentum of Helmut Thielicke's *Questions Christianity Addresses to the Modern World!* Men are swamped
by the radical relativization of modern life and are smother-
ing in sin; they exult in freedom without sensing that their
very license is under a curse; they live fast and furiously
without any quest for meaning and purpose; they are blind
to the final goal of all things. Shall we hide from them the
only message of recovery, the good news of God?

A deeper reason for the urgency of evangelism lies in the
imperative *now* which God has attached to the gospel. This
present life is the time of decision. No man who spurns the
opportunities for salvation in this life has reason to expect
new opportunities in the life to come; no man who turns a
deaf ear to God's call today has any guarantee to unending
opportunity tomorrow. The gospel of God is revocable; the
Spirit of God does not forever strive with man. The fourth
gospel affirms God's love for the world (3:16), but it declares also that those who do not believe are condemned,
condemned already (3:18). Written over the gospel is the
adverb "now," not the adverb "whenever." It has the life-or-
death urgency of a heart transplant, not the deferability of a
face-lifting which can be postponed year after year.

The more I read the arguments of men who affirm universal salvation, the less convinced I am of their fidelity to the
scriptural view. First, they must set a supposedly nonretri-
butive God of the New Testament against the admittedly
retributive God of the Old Testament. Then they must set a
supposed Jesus of unending mercy against the stern Jesus
of the "severe sayings" on final punishment, sayings which, it
should be noted, are fairly evenly distributed throughout

Mark, Q, L, and M, reputedly the main sources of the gospels. Then they must set the supposedly nonretributory passages in the epistles and the book of Revelation against the undeniably retributory passages. In other words, this artificial exegesis requires a Siamese-twin theology that can preserve universalism only by importing two Gods into the Bible and two Jesuses into the gospels.

The weight of the Bible is against automatic, inevitable or universal salvation. Through its enfeeblement of divine righteousness the theory implies a sentimental view of God, while through its exclusion of final punishment it implies a light view of moral guilt. What student of the gospels dares to say that sin can *never* be so terrible that it would not have been better had its perpetrator never been born, *never* so wicked that forgiveness is impossible either in this age or in the age to come (cf. Mk 3:29)? Or who dare say that the most reprehensible evil—whether the Nazi slaughter of the Jews or Judas' betrayal of Jesus—must evoke from God only a response of love? The Christ who said, "Come unto me" (Mt 11:28) also saw the coming judgment as a separation by the Son of man of men for the final doom of the wicked (Mt 25:31-46). The gospel has about it not only a human urgency, but also a divine urgency. *Today* is the day of God's salvation.

Only the modern misunderstanding of the church surpasses the modern misunderstanding of the gospel. For this misunderstanding the church has mainly herself to blame. For too many moderns, the church of Jesus Christ is essentially a building located on one city corner, housing a religious club whose members come once or twice a week in order to hear some professional lecturer develop a historical theme with a theological slant. Dues are collected weekly to keep the brick and mortar in good repair, to keep the lecturer physically capable of preparing his next discourse, and to enable denominational headquarters to keep accurate historical statistics.

Churches that fit this description are dying all around us, and the world is aware of it even if we are not. The June 15, 1969, London *Sunday Times* carried an article on "Dying Churches" that began: "The staunch, but ageing congregation of about five; the vicar's sad notice-board outside the church appealing for funds to save the steeple; the gravestones, disappearing under a jungle of weeds—depressing, but familiar landmarks all over England today."

We in America must take it as a judgment upon ourselves that so many churches have become a breeding place for doubt and that many who come week after week and year after year remain uncommitted to Christ. Thank God that our churches are not yet wholly forsaken, but surely they have themselves become mission fields. Failure to preach God's Word allows the world to make converts from the church's own ranks; it spawns divided souls and incipient nihilists in the very shadows of the pulpit and steeple. The church herself seems to be on the point of vanishing back into the world.

The real issue is whether we now hold Christianity in the form of a doomed modern compromise, a mixture of high ideals and clouded thoughts. Are we secretly unsure of ultimate truth and final destiny, so that church routines become for us a kind of sanctimonious humbug? Do we merely in a hope-against-hope manner desire a fate somehow different from that of which the nihilists speak, while we are no longer inwardly enlivened by the Christian hope? Can we no longer call upon the name of Jesus without stammering? Unless the gospel enlivens it, the church remains but another agitated segment of the world.

Men speak of the end of the modern world, and surely its supports are crumbling. Not only from the standpoint of the so-called "fourth man" who says he participates in no word or life of God, but also and especially from the perspective of the "new man" who knows the coming King, the modern world is giving way. Not the "fourth man," not the "man come of age," not the "postmodern man," but the man of Calvary holds the future secure in His hands. The church that lives in true union and daily fellowship with her risen Lord has no doubt about that.

The church of Jesus Christ is a company of men and women who view the past, present and future through God's plan of redemption. The living church knows herself to be rescued from the past, renewed in the present, and rewarded in the future.

First, the church knows herself as rescued from the world. The true church knows the forgiveness of sins and the reality of divine grace over against the demonic vitality of sin. She lives by the Spirit of God and exhibits a new style of life in the world; she knows herself as destined by God for a special future and stationed in the world for a special task.

Second, the church knows herself to be renewed in the present. To be sure, the church is not the kingdom of God in its completeness, but she is nothing if she is not the nearest approximation to God's kingdom which the earth has. How vain it is for the clergy to call the world to social justice and brotherhood if their own churches lack the marks of a fellowship of love and lag in the pursuit of righteousness. Through the lack of love and justice in her own ranks, the twentieth-century church herself may become a stone of stumbling. The church is but a mirage if she is not a concentrated manifestation of the obedience that marks God's kingdom.

Are our churches clearly the center of a new society, or have we scrapped true saintliness? Is it clear to the world that we are a corps waiting daily upon God for His briefing of the troops? Or do we seem like recruits who march briskly to whatever tune seems specially congenial to the times? Is it apparent that our goal is not simply the improvement of the ethos of humanity, but rather the rehumanization of man, indeed, the regeneration of man, and his transformation into the very image of Jesus Christ? The world dreads to open its morning newspaper; does the church still rejoice to open the Bible?

A runaway world is prone today to heap scorn on the church. The church's one authentic and irrefutable response is still a demonstration in word and deed of the great joy, the new freedom, the abundant life, that come by the holy power of Jesus Christ, who has already overcome the world.

For others the present may point to no sure future. For us, the past and present gain their grand climax, righteousness finds its ultimate vindication, hope turns to bright fulfillment, and faith becomes luminous sight, in the final consummation of all things. For the ascended Lord's return, the universal resurrection of the dead, the full conformity of believers to the image of God's Son, and the awesome victory of the kingdom of God and the terrible punishment of the impenitent, we expectantly wait.

In the gospel God has begun something in history that neither the world nor an apostate church can stop. That is why a church and world that play leapfrog with the gospel had best stop flirting with spiritual death, take the leap of biblical faith, and latch their destinies to the crucified and risen Lord who holds the future firmly in His hands.

13

When the Doors Are Locked

IF ANYTHING IS WORSE than being unexpectedly locked out, it is being unexpectedly locked in. Almost all of us, sometime or other, have been locked out of our homes or cars or offices by our forgetting the key, unwittingly locking a door on ourselves, or executing some other brilliant maneuver. But being locked in is even worse, particularly if one cannot get word to others and does not know when or whether rescue will come. One night in Monte Carlo, Mrs. Henry and I were trapped between floors in an elevator. We had not the faintest idea whether we would be there through the night or be released within the hour, as in fact we were.

No lock holds more terror than one which may be sealed forever. How we shudder to read of those coal-mine explosions in which workers are suddenly trapped underground! When survivors emerge, we hang onto their words to learn how their spirits died and revived a thousand times in those hours of uncertain hope.

Before I resigned full-time journalism to get a college education, the last story I covered for the New York *Herald-Tribune* turned on the misfortune of a Long Island worker who began digging a well on his birthday. His shovel-and-bucket operation had gotten him down about thirty feet when his wife called him for his birthday dinner. As he began to climb out, the walls caved in and he was buried under tons of earth. Was he perhaps cowering underground in an air pocket beside the ladder? Ambulance crews, fire departments, and derrick operators worked through the long night

101

digging a nearby well; people roosted in trees and watched through the night. Periodic cave-ins hampered the rescue effort. Everyone wondered what it was like inside that tomb —whether it was an endlessly approaching death or whether for that man on his birthday the end had already come, as, sad to say, it had.

If that birthday was turned into a burial, another burial was turned into a birthday—the day that Jesus Christ became "the first-begotten from the dead." On the evening of that very day the first disciples were gathered behind locked doors for fear of the Jews. They themselves were Jews, of course. Surely they especially feared the Sanhedrin, which had brought about the crucifixion of Jesus. Who would be next? Their fears were not ill-founded, as the violent persecutions reported in the book of Acts bear out.

These days I think a lot about the way the Christian church is bagged up and sacked in, moving on the margin of the modern mainstream, cut off from the formative cultural influences, restricted to the peripheral concerns of contemporary man. A Methodist district superintendent said recently, "There are 15 churches in my district; 12 could close down and the communities would not even miss them." That the same could be said of evangelical Christianity is tragic, for Evangelicalism, in its devotion to the biblical "good news," has the feel of authentic Christianity. We seem to be locked in by fear: not fear of the Jews, or fear of the Gentiles, or even a fear of God, but by an uncertain fear of ourselves, by lack of spiritual confidence, and by secret doubts. We evangelical Christians seem to be sealed off from the world by timidity, distrust, and a strange uncertainty about the Lord and what we expect from Him in the modern world. We gather less for buoyant fellowship than for conducting postmortems on our withering cause.

We cannot console ourselves with diatribes against institutional Christianity and the organized church. To be sure, institutional ecumenism is in deepening trouble; one respected religion reporter says privately that the National Council of Churches is now under such severe stress that he would not be surprised to see it go down. But evangelical independents are under too many pressures of their own to draw comfort from conciliar woes.

The backlash of black power is now being directed against specifically evangelical targets no less than against ecumenical denominations. Inflation of church-membership statistics is not a nonevangelical disease only. I find a decreasing percentage of young people in the church congregations, and when I ask pastors what they prefer me to speak on, they increasingly say, "Bring a word of encouragement to those who are present." Evangelical pastors are spending more and more time dispensing pep pills to spiritually anemic church members. We are being hedged in—and the world knows it, even if we may not.

Nobody is yet breathing out slaughter against evangelical Christians today, except perhaps in places like Red China. Pressures, restrictions, discriminations there are in Communist countries, and obstacles in lands like Egypt, Israel, Greece and Spain. But in the free world it is the Evangelicals who breathe out slaughter against one another: the American Council of Christian Churches against others; more recently, even Carl McIntire against the American Council; Bob Jones against Billy Graham; fundamentalists against Evangelicals, and Evangelicals against neo-Evangelicals.

One thing can be said for the early disciples: they were not slaughtering one another. Though it was in fear, they *were* united, and in that respect they even had an advantage over modern Evangelicals, who are divided into multitudinous factions. Each camp assures itself that it is God's chosen brigade for some coming lightning attack upon the crisis of our times. Each is confident that loyalty to it and its hierarchy and its institutions holds priority over what Evangelicals might do together. One wonders how much of the evangelical predicament of being confined to the fringes of modern life may be a penalty that Evangelicals are now paying for their own perversity. Make no mistake about it: the cost of evangelical division and dissension runs very high.

We have not learned lessons written large in church history; enemies of the truth exploit the vacuums created by our failure to stand together and our readiness to destroy one another's efforts. After he appealed to Caesar, the apostle Paul became execution bait because the Christians in Rome apparently divided over whether he ought ever to have carried his case to the emperor; at least Clement, one of the church Fathers, tells us this. Paul himself, in his letter to the Philippians from the Mamertine Prison, notes the tension and controversy among Christian workers in Rome. He writes of those who would "by personal rivalry, present Christ from mixed motives, meaning to stir up fresh trouble for me as I lie in prison" (Phil 1:17, NEB). Could this execution have been avoided had the early Christians stood united?

The week after the next atomic bomb falls, or after some great national tragedy, it will be far too late for Christians to stand together in magnificent witness; then we will have to cling to one another for sheer survival. Major decisions which we might have influenced bearing on the destiny of our neighbors and ourselves will already have been made. Would that we Evangelicals were not bagged up by a perverse self-satisfaction with our many divisions, but were huddled together instead in a real fear of failing to accomplish the mission our common Lord has given us.

It might not necessarily be an asset, but it would be less of a liability if we were locked in simply by fear of failure. We might then realize how wholly locked-up we are to God alone for any hopeful alternative to our present helplessness.

I can never forget something that happened during my years as editor of the *Port Jefferson Times-Echo* on Long Island. On a cold winter night on Long Island Sound a crew aboard a heavily loaded scow suddenly sensed that it was sinking. The seamen tried desperately to save it, but it was a losing battle; and when they noticed some piling thrusting out of the icy waters, they decided to jump overboard.

All through that blustery winter night they clung for life to that piling and cried out toward the blinking lights along the shore for help. In the morning some early fishermen saw them clinging to the piling, hands numb, some with frozen fingers, hardly alert to daybreak, and despairing of life. In the ensuing rescue the terrible irony of their experience became clear: all through that freezing night the men had clung for life to piling in water that was only four feet deep; at any moment of the night they could have walked safely to shore.

Something about evangelical fishing for men today raises again the image of those seamen clinging to the piling. Hemmed in by our anxieties, inhibitions and preoccupations, we little suspect that this may be the very moment to thrust into the terrifying waves of modernity, confident of the future of our cause.

What, after all, had huddled those early disciples together so that, instead of disappearing into the night and vanishing one by one into the Judean wilderness or taking their own lives in despair, they were companions knit together even in their fears? It was simply this: each one had come to know Jesus of Nazareth.

But the disciples did know, while we do not seem to, that God alone was the way out of their confining predicament. If they clung to the piling on a dark night, they knew that God alone is the bedrock beneath the billows on which they could hope to walk and run again.

To be locked in as Evangelicals could be a great asset if we discovered ourselves to be locked up to God for our very survival and if we made it our prime concern to mesh together in aggressive involvement with the world. We need to look far beyond evangelical personalities. Thank God for Billy Graham and any others that you care to place on the same list. But they are nothing, and we are nothing, if God does not come to us in our need and give life and blessing.

We need creative new ventures in the future—an institute for advanced Christian studies, one or more Christian universities, a school of creative and communicative arts, cassette or taped lecture series covering the whole curriculum of Christian studies, and on and on. But none of these projects will mean any more than our present programs on the present basis. No strategy can carry the cause of Jesus Christ adequately in the modern world unless the risen Christ is present in person to smash our hesitations and reservations and inhibitions and to set us free for the world as we ought to be free.

During my year of research in Cambridge, England, I discovered one morning that my Cortina was locked in the garage and heaven alone had any inkling where the one garge key was. What good is a car—or a cause, for that matter—however powerful it may be, when it is behind locked doors and nobody has a key to get it in motion? I called the police (many people today think law and order holds the answer to all problems), but even they could not help. The heavy iron hinges and overlapping flanges on those garage doors had held fast for fifty years; a friend and I were soon convinced that they were not about to give way on this particular morning.

Our downstairs neighbor was a brilliant woman, professor of mathematics in Cambridgeshire College of Technology and Arts, and she joined us when she heard the commotion. She suggested that I get a hammer and screwdriver while she looked over the situation. When I returned, she said, "Put the screwdriver there, hit it for all you are worth, and let's see what happens." To the amazement of everyone except her, the doors threw themselves wide open. She knew the secret of where and what power needed to be applied.

So it was with those early disciples who had huddled behind locked doors for fear of the outside world. The risen Lord appeared to them, and He knew what power needed to be applied and where. His power did not simply spring open locked doors, but accelerated their arrested hearts. Jesus, who died and was alive again, showed them His hands and His side and said "Peace"—a peace that has no fear of death, a peace that knows the power and love of God, a peace that the world cannot give. Jesus gave that fearful clutch of disciples His peace, and He gave them His commission: "Go into all the world and preach the gospel." Then He breathed the Holy Spirit upon them. In this gift of the Holy Spirit lay the birthday of the church. Jesus knew what and where divine power needed to be applied, and the doors to the world swung wide again.

When we live with slammed doors, shut doors, sealed doors, we need nothing so much as to hear the voice of Him who calls: "I am he that liveth, and was dead. . . . I . . . have the keys of hell and of death" (Rev 1:18). If we are going to find apostolic momentum in the modern world, we need to be reminded that this age is already under fire from the age to come, that God's appointed Judge has already been openly identified, and that we are on personal speaking terms with the coming King. When we are bagged up and sacked in, no better cure exists for spiritual claustrophobia than to renew our vows to the risen Christ.

There are in the United States today tens of thousands, even hundreds of thousands, of Evangelicals who are waiting for some courageous voice to rally them to a new and bolder course of action. They are distressed by the stance of ecumenical Christianity, disturbed over denominational trends, dismayed at the impotence of Evangelicals in their present divisions. Tens of hundreds of thousands feel this way. They sense that if things drift along as they are, soon our dissent will mean nothing; it is now or never for an evangelical thrust that can still make a difference.

The new hour must begin sometime and somewhere if it is to strike at all. And the way for it to begin is for some to fall on their knees and to confess: "We are locked in by fear, fear of man, fear of ourselves, fear of everything but God. We need desperately to be locked up to God, to God alone, so the doors to the world may fling open again, and Christ's 'Go ye' be a blessed release rather than a vexing burden."

I am not much given to writing prayers, though I have long been in the word business. Many good prayers have been written, and all too few are being said. But one day I happened upon words from the general confession in the Lord's Supper as Methodists observe it: "We acknowledge and bewail our manifold sins and wickedness. . . . We are heartily sorry for our misdoings, the remembrance of them is grievous to us. . . . We do earnestly repent. . . . Have mercy, have mercy, forgive us all that is past, and may we hereafter . . ." That, I submit, is the right kind of prayer for Evangelicals behind locked doors. Hardly will they say "may we hereafter" than, like those early disciples, they will find the risen one at their side to shape the future.

14

Is It Too Late for the Church?

ONE QUESTION has haunted me ever since the Asia-South
Pacific Congress on Evangelism (Singapore, 1968): Is it
possible that we Western Christians are right now forfeiting
our last great opportunity for a worldwide witness to Jesus
Christ?

Today much more than technology, tourism, and secular
morality is moving from West to East. The very population
balance is shifting to Asia. In fact, two-thirds of the world's
people—two billion persons—now live in Asia. India and
Pakistan alone have more inhabitants than the United States,
Canada, and Latin America combined.

Asia's outstripping of the Western world in population
comes at a time when the Western missionary, for various
reasons, is fast losing his toehold in the Orient. What's more,
almost half of Asia's two billion souls now live in countries
actually sealed off from evangelism. Mainland China alone
isolates 825 million persons—one-quarter of the whole human
race.

Despite missionary retrenchment and despite the dilution
of Christianity in the West, Asian Christians, thank God,
have no intention of permitting the name of Christ to be cen-
sored even in China. Christians in Asia are looking beyond
the seemingly hopeless atheistic future of this colossal nation to implement the Lord's commission to "go . . . and make
disciples of all nations" (Mt 28:19, RSV). Throughout Asia,
Christian refugees pray regularly for a reopening of the doors

109

of mainland China to the gospel. Indeed, many ask God to send a disunifying spirit upon China's leaders that will snap their stranglehold on the masses. Many Asians know first-hand what befell Christians and the churches of North Korea and mainland China when totalitarianism overtook them. One delegate to the Asian Congress on Evangelism was number three on the Communists' list for slaughter if they had retained their grip on Indonesia. Many believers hail the growing tensions between Peking and Russia, Peking and Asia, Peking and Africa, Russia and Eastern Europe, and inside mainland China itself as a preliminary answer to their prayers. Displaced Chinese Christians think plans should even now be made for evangelization of post-Communist mainland China; they believe that divine providence and prayer remain more vital forces in modern history than Marxist motifs.

At present such traditional methods of evangelism as public proclamation, Christian schools and hospitals are obviously not permitted in mainland China. The only means of access now are a few inroads from a distance, particularly the radio work of Far East Broadcasting Company, which penetrates behind the Bamboo Curtain with the gospel. Asian Christians are convinced that literature in the simple Mandarin language should now be in preparation. It was the Communists who introduced Mandarin as the unified spoken language which all under the age of thirty can understand; 300 million adults now read and write it. Commenting that the disciples once lowered a needy person through the roof of a house, one Asian worker observed, "We have learned that if the front door is closed, windows and back doors sometimes remain open."

But Asian Christians are praying as well for a renewed Christian witness in North Korea, North Vietnam, Burma, Tibet and other restricted areas. In South Vietnam right now plans are in the making for a massive evangelistic thrust as soon as peace negotiations permit; special emphasis will fall on lay evangelism and child evangelism.

In actual numbers Asian Christians represent only 3 percent of the population. But this fact does not deter them; they are alive to their evangelistic duty and privileges, terrible obstacles notwithstanding. While Western Christians despite their greater numbers and resources seem to be indifferent to what may be their last global evangelistic opportunity, Asian evangelists are accelerating the thrust begun by men like William Carey, Adoniram Judson, and Hudson Taylor.

In taking up the burden of Asian evangelism they are neither antiwhite nor anti-Western. To be sure, they see no need for further transplantation and imposition of Western architecture, art and music. And they sense the dangers of ecumenical syncretism, German theology, and emerging patterns of British and American morality. Buoyed to fresh confidence by remembering that "the first Adam was an Asian, and so was the Second," the Asian Christians are determined that God's grace in Christ shall not be lost or go amiss in their land.

Is it too late? Is the cause still a viable one? Are not both the world and the church outrunning the gospel at a hopelessly discouraging pace? Can one any longer speak of Christian evangelism in global terms? Would it not be far easier to postulate a universal and cosmic redemption in Christ which removes the burden of a particular message to three billion people? Do we not switch Christianity onto a provincial siding if we insist on personal evangelical decision? After all, the mere logistics of such a requirement stagger the mind, let alone our missionary resources.

What's more, just how sure is institutional Christianity today of its mission in the world? And are not influential ecumenical theologians seriously divided over the ground and content of Christian belief? Can the church still face the world with the New Testament message unrevised and un-demythologized? Is it still possible, or is it too late, to call men and women everywhere to personal faith in the crucified and risen Christ?

The World Congress on Evangelism (Berlin, 1966) convened at a crucial crossroads in church and world history to weigh the evangelistic mandate. From it issued a call for evangelical obedience to the Great Commission that is being heard in land after land. At Berlin were gathered not denominational or ecclesiastical leaders as such, nor even missionaries serving in distant lands; in attendance, rather, were nationals from around the globe who in their countries bear the burden of evangelism as a Christian imperative. Whether the Berlin Congress inaugurated a turning point in evangelical Christianity remains to be seen. It has already inspired similar congresses in Africa, Asia, the United States, and Canada.

What was strategic about the setting of the World Congress on Evangelism?

First, the congress was chronologically significant. It was held at the threshold of the last third of the twentieth century, when half the world population lives under political atheism and the other half yields increasingly to the pressures of secular materialism and sensate culture. The congress convened at the beginning of a generation which will live to see the world population double itself; three-fourths of the people now living will be alive to greet the twenty-first century, and by the year 2000 the world population will be twice what it is now. The congress was held in the space age and the age of mass media. Many who came to Berlin had never before traveled by air; coming thousands of miles overnight, they were jolted into awareness of how swiftly the gospel could in fact be carried to the ends of the earth.

Second, the congress was ecumenically significant. It demonstrated "cooperative Christianity" on a basis that superseded the question of affiliation with the World Council of

Churches or any other organization. The delegates, from one hundred nations and belonging to seventy-six church bodies, represented both mainstream denominations within the conciliar movement and other groups outside the World Council. Participating churches went back historically as far as the Mar Thoma Church, which traces its beginnings in India to the apostle Thomas; others were young churches in Africa and Asia. The youngest of all to participate was the Auca Church in Latin America so recently sprung from the work of five American missionary martyrs. Special speakers included Emperor Haile Selassie, titular head of the Coptic Church in Ethiopia, a twice-born Christian who implored delegates to get on with the evangelistic task.

Racial and national differences were put aside in Christ. One evening while a Congolese delegate was telling how his people had been led to Christ, one of the Auca Indians ran down the aisle, jumped to the platform, and embraced a new-found Christian brother from another of the world's remote jungles. It was a moving, spontaneous display of evangelical ecumenism.

Third, the congress was ecclesiastically significant. For an entire generation worldwide church assemblies and conferences had been held on such issues as church union, faith and order, church and society, but none had concerned itself specially with implementing and fulfilling the Great Commission. Today the Christian community represents only 28 percent of the world population and is clearly a diminishing remnant; yet assemblies of the World Council of Churches and meetings of the Vatican Council have had other priorities. Because many leaders claim to speak for the church while they have lost an understanding of the gospel and often are more concerned for other causes than they are for evangelism, the Berlin Congress called the churches to evangelization as the Christian's inescapable duty. At a time when secular religionists were asking whether the church had out-lived its usefulness and even some Evangelicals felt that

evangelism was almost synonymous with Billy Graham crusades, the congress gave global vision and impetus to evangelism. It encouraged worldwide proclamation of a prospect
for peace and purity, for hope and happiness, which men and
women and children of all races and lands may personally
share.

Fourth, the congress was theologically significant. It sought
to set evangelism in the context of serious theology and to
enliven theology with a sense of evangelistic urgency. The
standing ovation given to Professor Johannes Schneider of
Germany for his appraisal of recent theological deviations
attested the delegates' awareness that the health of biblical
evangelism is determined by biblical theology. Loss of a
scriptural theology, they knew, brings loss of a biblical definition of evangelism; vigorous evangelical witness requires
evangelist-theologians and theologian-evangelists. A message that enlists only man's will for Christ while it leaves the
mind unpersuaded leaves its converts vulnerable to every
vagrant ideology. In calling the churches back to the Bible
and to the biblical mandate, the Berlin Congress set the task
of evangelism within the framework of revealed religion and
the truth of God.

Fifth, the congress was socially significant. It correlated
the evangelistic imperative with the specific trends and concerns of the contemporary world. While the congress did not
share the view of the political clergy, who emphasize the task
of changing social structures more than concern for the conversion of individuals to Christ, it was not on that account
asleep to the modern social crisis. From the congress came
not only the strongest statement on race yet approved by any
evangelical gathering, but also a list of six strategic areas for
evangelical engagement in the closing third of this century.
These are:

The great cities with their high-rise jungles so impervious
to penetration from outside. Cities by the year 2000 may
stretch 200 miles and, by their impact on the mass media and

their influence on the masses, will shape the spirit and life of whole nations.

The student world, particularly the 20 million college and university students of today. The leaders of the Protestant Reformation were university-trained men. What the next generation thinks and does will be determined largely by the convictions the young intellectuals around us now are acquiring. Among today's students are tomorrow's leaders, not only in the ministry, but also in politics, education, the mass media, literature, the arts, and the sciences. What are we doing to reach them—even fifty of them, or ten, or one? In the United States there are 3,000 Christian bookstores. Until recently, when a group of Christians decided something should be done about it, less than a dozen bookstores were located adjacent to the large universities. The student world is a crucial target for evangelization.

The mass media of newspapers, magazines, books, radio and television. The challenge and responsibility the mass media present are staggering, to say the least. In the United States alone some 40,000 paperback titles are now available; sales run $350 million a year. But American books are expensive for the British reader, and British books, in turn, are very expensive for Asian readers. With the increase in literacy, Asian Evangelicals are pleading for Christian literature. Who will provide it? It is sobering to learn that in today's age of mass media, the Christian remnant is addressing its literature not to the multitudes beyond, but to those who are already Christians. Even the Latin America Mission, one of the better evangelical societies, discovered that only 4 percent of its literature was aimed toward the non-Christian world.

C. S. Lewis was one of this century's most gifted Christian writers. Suppose at a cost of about £800 ($2,000) a full-page Christmas or Easter message by Lewis could have appeared in a London newspaper and thus gone to 3½ million readers. Would not this have been a strategic and economical use of his talents? How many years would it take a clergyman to get the same message across to as many seldom-go-to-church prospects? We all know that today the motion pictures, radio and television have overwhelming influence on the masses. Are we training evangelical youth for these mass-media opportunities? Are we using the mass media that often cost us nothing, or surrendering them by default to far-out cults or quacks? What most distinguishes the twentieth century from the first century, said someone at Singapore, are the mass media and space travel. Both these developments, he added, can be used to spread the gospel to the whole world.

Technology, particularly the computer. Scientists engaged in aerospace projects and in programing can teach us a great deal about computerized research and how to coordinate information for facilitating world evangelism. In the United States there is now a research center that computerizes the answers given by evangelical scholars to a vast range of questions and problems. Soon this material will be available by inexpensive leased-wire hookup to students on evangelical campuses in any part of the nation. If we are to claim all contemporary culture for Christ, we shall need even to computerize for the glory of God. In church life and church growth much that has been learned in one context can be helpful in another; every tool that promotes evangelical effectiveness should be used to the full.

Social concern. Whatever touches man's humanity is a legitimate concern of the Christian. Social justice has become a household word. We must not simply emphasize how the Marxists distort it; we must declare that the biblical demand for social righteousness is what first released this vision into the world. Moreover, we need to relate the modern aspiration for social justice to the judgment of God upon men and nations, to the redemption that is in Christ Jesus, and to the daily obedience God requires of us all. Those who regard politics as the modern form of evangelism need not beguile us. On the other hand, we dare not plead evangelism as an excuse for neglecting our duty in the sociopolitical realm, especially today when any minority in the free world has the right to press the claims of righteousness upon the public order. In its most influential epochs the church has been as fully interested in justice as in theology and evangelism. Law and politics offer decisively important vocational opportunities for evangelical young people.

The role of the layman. Someone has estimated that on the basis of recent church statistics in the United States, it now takes six pastors and 1,000 laymen to win one person to Christ in a single year. This discovery has jarred American laymen to fresh evangelistic vigor. The crisis in evangelism today does not stem primarily from the fact that many who claim to speak for the church do not know what the church is or what it stands for. The deeper, true crisis is the fact that those who rightly know their responsibility for fulfilling the Lord's Great Commission are not actively doing so. What gain is it to spend our energy criticizing churchmen who conform the gospel to the thought patterns of our age, if we ourselves do not confront modern man with the gospel? Samuel Johnson once remarked that "no sensible man speaks of his religion." But in our time insensible and nonsensical men are speaking much about strange faiths; for Christians to reduce God's grace in Christ to something unmentionable can only breed doubts about revealed religion.

The question "Is it too late for the church?" cannot be answered by an abstract assessment of the contemporary religious scene. It is a question each of us answers by the measure of our love for Christ and for those who do not know Him. Do we consider it unworthy of mention to those at our side that Christ is risen from the dead, and that the Holy Spirit gives new life? Do we each day ask ourselves whether Jesus Christ truly reigns in us as Saviour and Lord, or whether we are hesitant disciples in bondage to the sin of silence? Are we Western Christians as a whole forfeiting our

last great opportunity for a world witness to Jesus Christ because of indifference and unconcern for the souls of men?
If the light of Christianity flickers lower and lower in the
West, so that the names of Darwin and Freud and Marx and
Einstein wholly eclipse the name of Jesus Christ, who will
be to blame: vociferous propagandists for the modern mood
or silent followers of the Nazarene?

If Christ be not risen, said the apostle Paul, we are false
witnesses of God. Presumably, it never occurred to him that
men for whom Christ died and who know Him as risen from
the dead might not be witnesses at all.

15

God Speaks in Renewal

NUMBERS of our American cities are miring in savagery. With moral absolutes obscure if not disowned, young and old alike steep themselves in prurience and grovel in a shadow culture of drugs, drink and debauchery. Life for many people, as our great news magazines reflect it, has little meaning and purpose. Many now consider work distasteful, saving for the future unrewarding, reflective education a dispensable diversion, sport or travel our highest creative engagement, political protest the chief expression of democracy, and war a worse evil than loss of freedoms. Others stand silent, unaroused by flagrant lawlessness, by nations' systematically scorching one another with bombs, or by our generation's polluting of the only planet we know whereon human life is possible. Across the earth the human family is divided against itself. Multitudes die of famine, myriads are barred from justice because of prejudice, and throngs are exiled from neighbor love because of pigment. Science is often most welcome for its aid in exploiting the earth or in destroying nearby nations.

If churches and synagogues still consider themselves custodians of people's values, they must acknowledge that in this age no follower of the ancient prophets or of Jesus of Nazareth can any longer afford to be proud. They must openly admit their failure to inform the mind and will of this generation.

Or does not God today have an argument also with the churches? Who of us has the righteousness requisite for ad-

ministering ecclesiastical tongue lashings in His name? Do
we not all share the guilt of looking on passively in a world
gone wild? Does not God's voice call every last one of us up
short because we church members, too, share the pathologies
of modern life? Do not we, like our unchurched neighbors,
sleep all too soundly through the weeping and wailing of the
oppressed?

God is calling to modern churchianity, even calling out
against it for its lethargy and hardheartedness. Today, as
ever, the church's one sure road to renewal is a direct return
to God's three R's—repentance, regeneration and regathering.

Renewal is not some possibility latent within us; the
church has no magical capacity for self-renewal. Renewal is
not some stratagem we devise; it comes as a divine gift. Without divine renewal, the church is trapped in the status quo
of the present, cut off from the best of the past and from the
kingdom of God and from a hopeful future. Without divine
renewal the so-called church reverts swiftly into the world.

Repentance is the first ingredient of authentic renewal. By
her repentance the church confesses that she is not the origi-
nator of renewal but the needy object of it. Repentance
means open acknowledgment of our wrong and presently un-
promising ways. Repentance is earnestly seeking God's forgiveness for ourselves, our pastors, our denominational administrators—indeed, for the whole people of God.

W. A. Visser 't Hooft warned the ecumenical community a
decade and a half ago that there is "no renewal without repentance." His words are still waiting for takers. "All great
renewals in the history of the church," he wrote, "have been
movements of repentance."[1] At the forepart of the first century, Jesus' message in the gospels to the Jews was repentance; at the century's close in the book of Revelation, repentance stands at the center of the risen One's message to the
churches.

Repentance pledges our abiding dependence upon God;
God alone, it concedes, can renew us. If for us God has be-

come irrelevant or is simply to be taken for granted, then our brand of Christianity, or churchmanship, is tunneling headlong to hell. Some buffoons say audibly as well as in their hearts, "There is no God" (Ps 14:1), and these few misguided intellectuals dare to plant themselves in churches and seminaries and religious publishing houses. Worse yet, legions of impious God-deserting church members, the Lord have mercy, no longer pray and search the Scriptures. Is it any wonder some consider racism their divine right, war a divine necessity, poverty a divine punishment, justice a human impracticality, and love a Christian elective?

We desperately need a tidal wave of repentance and a fresh inundation of God's forgiveness. What claim, what right have we to be called Christians if we conceal our dependence on God? Or welcome formulas for radical social change that dismiss the reality of God as inconsequential? Or invoke God's name only as an honorific preface to our modern sociological theorizing? Or confer on Jesus the title "Nazarene Revolutionary" in order to lend a sacred mystique to our own political preferences? We get things out of order; we put man before his Maker, when concern for renewal of the church is thought to be first and foremost a concern for restructuring the world.

Some Christians consider a call to repentance tolerable enough provided its real meaning is social involvement and political engagement. The nitty-gritty, as they see it, is the plunge into the world, and if for the sake of social action they must endure a pious prologue, then let the sermon be short and sweet. We need to challenge this externalistic, environmental approach to God's kingdom. After all, Christ's demand for a new order probes to the very core of man himself. Of God's indispensable three R's for renewal, repentance comes first.

Rebirth is the second of God's three R's. Rebirth generates the first breath of kingdom life and is the Open sesame! to

God's new order. In rebirth God shapes in a man a new conscience and a new character; He shapes a new sensitivity to personal needs and a new devotion to public justice. God seeks not only a new man, but also a new society, a new heavens and earth; His kingdom is not simply internal, and it does not lack social perspective. He who finds new life in Christ is exhorted both to pray and to activate the petition, "Thy kingdom come. Thy will be done in earth, as it is in heaven" (Mt 6:10).

The annals of man contain no parallel to the transformation Christianity has wrought in the West, and the world today has a right to expect from Christians more than it sees. At the same time, the modern world expects from the church what it has no right to expect, namely, a sociopolitical utopia divorced from moral and spiritual commitments. This Christianity does not promise. It is time the church stopped speaking of the new covenant in terms of social legislation only, set the vision of a new society in its true Messianic context, and got back to the commandments of God and the gospel of Christ.

Philosophers in ancient Greece and Rome wrote at length about justice and peace in society; yet those great empires collapsed for lack of the will to do the right, and confusion over the right thing to do. No new society of righteousness can be successfully grafted onto a race of unregenerates, and no civilization that spurns moral imperatives will long endure. God's commandments still offer the profoundest wisdom that churchmen can bring to the modern political world, and the gospel of Christ still offers the most potent dynamic for actualizing these commandments in daily life.

To promote justice and to restrain disorder in our fallen society, God wills civil government. Many of our social problems—notably those of war and civil rights—cannot be solved apart from just governments; others, like pollution, are unlikely to be solved without some governmental restraints. Just governments require just laws; just laws, in turn, are demanded and observed only by just citizens and are fully enforced only by just rulers.

Christianity has every biblical reason for insisting that government should go the very last mile as an instrument of justice, and for challenging every citizen to be politically active to the full limit of his ability and competence. One would think, however, that twentieth-century Christianity would not fail to say as much about the lack of political freedom and human rights under totalitarian regimes as about the need of political participation and justice in our own land. The special, long-range contribution of Christianity to the sociopolitical arena is its emphasis on the limits of government and on the state's answerability to God as the source, stipulator, and ultimate sanction of all human rights and duties.

Does this mean the church is required to speak only in moral abstractions and must venture no specific responses to the burning issues of American society, for example, the Vietnam War and poverty? Not at all.

At stake for the church in the conflicts of Asia and the Middle East is the issue of just-versus-unjust war. Unless the whole rationale of war is seriously debated, the churches will be as ignorant of the basic issues when the next war begins as when the present one ends. Is it not clear that an aggressor indulged is an aggressor encouraged? Again, have churches which are truly persuaded that any and every war is unjust, any option but to recognize civil disobedience as just, unless the government has made adequate provision for conscientious objectors? And when churchmen discourage youth from carrying guns in Asia, have not Christians a right to ask whether they prepare them to carry bandages and Bibles there instead—or are Christian activists content simply to fuel the fires of political protest?

Happily, the dichotomy between evangelism and social concern has broken down; today controversy in the churches centers rather on what constitutes **authentic** Christian social action. We may differ over how best to respond, but respond we must, when reportedly the proportion of black poverty in our land is almost four times greater than white, 40.6 per cent alongside 11.9 percent. We must do something when an average black family's income is only 58 percent that of an average white family's, and declining, and black unemployment is more than twice that of white unemployment.

I do not think Washington is the first place the church should run to for solutions; she is free to take creative, voluntary actions herself. Were every church in America to adopt one poverty-stricken family or one unemployed church member and surround him with warm human relationships while conducting a joint search for solutions, Christians would make a notable dent in the poverty problem. The problems of our big cities are especially acute, but they are not on that account insurmountable. Swift liaison between white and black churches could produce creative voluntary means for alleviating them, particularly if the massive labor unions would likewise become directly involved on a voluntary basis.

Law plays a necessary role in fallen society, and Christians no less than non-Christians need the law to remind them of their public duties. In our lifetime some very desirable legislative changes have come about. The social gospel need not be credited for them; some of its dubious specifics, like legislated prohibition, have long since been undone. For all that, the basic obstruction to human community is the problem of sin; particularly, efforts to establish community are undercut by sin, which perverts personal relationships. Our style of Christianity does not deserve to survive unless it intensifies and purifies personal relationships. We must show the world again that this is Christianity's superlative excellence.

In 1933, while a young newspaperman on Long Island, I became a Christian. On every hand, churchmen then were enthusiastic for the new social gospel, which, they said, would usher in the kingdom of God through progressive social legislation. This gradual leavening of the democratic process has proceeded year after year; yet at the end of a whole generation we are still as far from the kingdom as ever. Nor will any radical, revolutionary politico-economic program establish God's kingdom, however much its measures be dignified as the will of God. In recent decades the legislative wineskins many churchmen have been patching wear and tear swiftly and show the need for continuing repair. Is it not time for the church to spend less time patching old wineskins and to offer men around us a taste of new wine?

Neither the revolutionaries nor the hippies offer a viable alternative to the status quo. Both thrive on protest against a rotting society; neither has a workable solution. Many hippies are irrelevant enough to be comic, many revolutionaries irrational enough to be tragic. Those who borrow the slogan "Revolution *ahne Zwang*" (revolution without force) are woefully misled, for revolution is bloody business; it is no Sunday school picnic. To say that revolution has become a necessary part of our times confers needless dignity on lawlessness and irrationalism. The place to find a viable alternative to the status quo is still in the revealed will of God, for the only sure thing about efforts to remedy a rotten society without God is that conditions will get worse, not better. God's way to renewal is repentance and regeneration; these are two of God's supreme gifts to mankind.

God's third R for renewal is regathering. The Christian movement *was* ordained to shape a strategic social witness. But it has a responsibility to maintain the emphasis where it belongs, namely, on the personal element in the human community under God, rather than on impersonal structures. What divine irony that while the organized church is concentrating on world structures as the key to the kingdom, God is shaking and rattling the structures of the institutional church!

Regathering means new intrapersonal relationships looking toward a new heaven, and a new earth under God, who makes all things new; it is reconciliation in depth. Regathering is the evidence of our reconciliation: regathered to God from our prodigality, regathered to one another from our animosity. Regathering sees God's redemption primarily in reconciled persons. It does not mean escaping from multiculture churches to clannish exclusivism, or fleeing from black urban areas to white suburban temples; nor does it mean simply reconvening in the same old way under the old conditions. Reconciliation puts men on new speaking and living terms with God and with their neighbors near and far.

Regathering is the answer to both spiritual individualism and social isolationism. It aligns the regenerate person's life and mission with the corporate fellowship of believers; it overcomes the barriers men have built around themselves. On the one hand, it emphasizes the gathering of the community of believers with their invisible risen Lord for worship, searching the Scripture, prayer, and instruction. Regathering stresses the ready acceptance of God's claim on each individual member for the sake of the whole body of Christ. On the other hand, it emphasizes no less the Christian community's involvement in the life and fortunes of the whole family of man.

Regathering breaks the clergy out of hierarchical superiority and lifts the whole people of God to spiritual priesthood and vocational responsibility in God's service. It resists anything—denominational, antidenominational, or conciliar—that identifies Christians to the world as an organizational lump. Organizations crumble, thereby mirroring division even while posing unity. Regathering finds in the already existing oneness guaranteed by the living Lord the most effective bond for Christian unity.

Regathering is ecumenical in the finest sense; on the local level it enlists believers everywhere for worship, fellowship and mission, not on the basis of buildings and hierarchies, but on the sole basis of Christ and the Bible. All too long have church buildings kept Christians apart in a supposedly ecumenical age. Regathering brings together all in the local community who are truly Christ's, whatever their color, culture, or conciliar striations. A hundred people faithfully on their knees in prayer in each of a thousand cities across America may mean more in the long run for the church and the world than costly global gatherings.

Seeking to impress the modern world either by sheer massiveness or by donning revolutionary armor is unbecoming the church of Christ. Christ's church should herald the full-bodied truth of revelation and the new freedom, righteousness, and joy of life in Christ. As the new society that privately and publicly owns Christ as coming King, the regathered community by the Spirit's enabling should project in microcosm the standards and life of the kingdom of God.

In some areas pastors may well dispense with ailing Sunday night services, forsaken prayer meetings, and endless committee meetings to enable concerned Christians to meet with neighbors in their homes for repentance and renewal gatherings. Churches deserve no credit for perpetuating venerable traditions to which multitudes are indifferent, when there are new and more vital ways of enlisting them for the gospel. Morphological fundamentalism is no evangelical asset. Ten years from now pastors may be walking among the ghost towns of what they once hoped would become temples of the Holy Ghost, and they may recall the words of Jesus: "Behold, your house is left unto you desolate" (Mt 23:38).

Why should not ten small churches, struggling to meet their budgets and reaching fewer and fewer people, dissolve into a corporate Christian FM radio station with a united voice to the community, and at the same time enlist young people in mass-media witness? Is there no reason for a strategically located church with dwindling attendance to become a Christian reading and literature center with lectures and discussion groups on the Christian classics as well as the Bible? Might not another become a social service or youth

center? Another might become a center for creative leisure
that provides instruction in music and the arts and in writing,
with the aim of enlisting evangelical youth at these frontiers,
for Christians have a stake in the world of culture. Might yet
another become a great downtown center for Bible exposition, prophetic study, expository preaching, and even Bible-
study extension courses?

Ten years from now we may sadly wonder why we did not
regather our resources of people and talents in order to match
them to the needs of the community around us. Will we
wonder then why it seemed so imperative now to perpetuate
ancient routines and time-worn forms while people around
us are spiritually starving and dying? Will we wonder then
why our stake in mortgaged buildings and denominational
patriotism and retirement benefits detoured us from the
mainstream of history on the move?

The Christian vanguard needs to regather for the sake of
the world, for life and witness and mission in the world. Let
us penetrate the world with a witness to the commandments
of God and strive to bring all realms of culture and life under
His healing hand. We have a mandate, loud and clear, to
preach the commands of God and to live by these commands.
Let us make the commandments of God so clear that the
world will tremble and reach for new life. Let us translate
them through persuasion and example into historical realities.

16

The Barbarians Are Coming

WE LIVE IN THE TWILIGHT of a great civilization, amid the deepening decline of modern culture. Those strange beast-empires of the books of Daniel and Revelation seem already to be stalking and sprawling over the surface of the earth. Only the success of modern science hides us from the dread terminal illness of our increasingly technological civilization.

Because our sights are fixed on outer space and man on the moon, we cannot see the judgment that hangs low over our own planet. We applaud modern man's capability but forget that nations are threatening each other with atomic destruction, that gunsmoke darkens our inner cities, and that our near neighbors walk in terror by day and sleep in fear by night. We sit glued to television sets, unmindful that ancient rulers staged circuses to switch the minds of the restless ones from the realities of a spiritually vagrant empire to the illusion that all was basically well.

We are so steeped in the anti-Christ philosophy—namely, that success consists in embracing not the values of the Sermon on the Mount but an infinity of material things, sex, and status—that we little sense how much of what passes for practical Christianity is really an apostate compromise with the spirit of the age.

Our generation is lost to the truth of God, to the reality of divine revelation, to the content of God's will, to the power of His redemption, and to the authority of His Word. For this loss it is paying dearly in a swift relapse to paganism.

129

The savages are stirring again; you can hear them rumbling and rustling in the tempo of our times.

The barbarians are coming. All our scientific achievements can be misused by those coming barbarians for their cruel ends. Hitler and the Nazis have already employed twentieth-century know-how to cremate people by the hundreds of thousands. Their gas chambers were highly efficient. Stalin and other tyrants learned long ago that captive mass media could enslave myriads of modern men. Red Chinese warlords seem eager to play with atomic fire, although the bombs that fell on Hiroshima and Nagasaki were but miniversions of our current maxiweapons.

Year by year the probability of a globally destructive nuclear war increases. The Nobel prizeman George Wald, a renowned biologist, in a speech at Massachusetts Institute of Technology cited a distinguished professor of government at Harvard who calculates the accelerating odds for a full-scale nuclear war to be one chance in three by 1990, one chance in two by the year 2000. All our scientific know-how can be deployed for destructive ends.

The barbarians are coming. Reason and persuasion are giving way to mob pressure and revolution as the approved means of social change. Anyone can play this game of compulsion if he has enough social dynamite. But the price is another nail in the coffin for democratic processes. Down the road are the approaching caravans of the Machiavellis and Leviathans and those might-makes-right despots.

Colleges and universities are faltering as the intellectually critical centers of society; some have even become launching pads for social anarchy. The confusion and chaos of society have moved onto the campuses and into the classrooms of our schools; in the name of democratic pluralism, major educational institutions forsake the name of God, and pride themselves on academic excellence while they neglect objective truth, disagree on ultimate values, and bend to the anti-intellectualistic temper of our times.

In *Enemies of the Permanent Things*, Russell Kirk puts the modern predicament this way: "The fountains of the great deep seem to be broken up in our time. Institutions that have endured for a millennium are awash, and the surly question before us, is whether the whole fabric of civilization can survive the present rate of economic and social alteration."[1]

The barbarians are coming. Institutional Christianity has dropped the last barricade to the return of the pagan man; preoccupied with the changing of social structures, it muffles the call for a new humanity and, in doing so, forfeits a mighty spiritual opportunity at the crossroads of modern history. The organized church that ought to have been burdened for the evangelization of the earth has been too busy powdering her nose to preserve an attractive public image or powdering the revolutionaries and reactionaries who need rather to be remade in Christ's image.

Disillusionment over organized Christianity is soaring; one can see it in the declining statistics on church attendance and in diminishing denominational giving and in second thoughts about the ecumenical projection of one great world church. While ecumenists stress that the strides toward church union commend Christ to the world, a whole generation is growing up with no awareness of regeneration by the Holy Spirit. A species without clear ideas about sin and sacrilege, a race for whom God and the supernatural are virtually eclipsed, this generation comprises individuals with no interest in the *imago Dei*, earthlings with no eternal concerns.

The forerunners of these half-men are being nourished wherever a pulpit no longer preaches the commandments of God and the sinfulness of man, the ideal humanity of Jesus Christ and the divine forgiveness of sins, and the fact of saving grace. Obscure the vital tenets of revealed religion, detour churchgoers from piety and saintliness, and in the so-called enlightened nations multitudes will soon relapse to a retrograde morality, churchgoers will live in Corinthian immorality, churchmen will encourage situational ethics, and the line between the Christian and the worldling will scarcely be found. Even in the church, barbarians are breeding: beware, the Scripture says, of the lawless one who will occupy the temple of God (2 Th 2:4). Savages are stirring the dust of a decadent civilization and already slink in the shadows of a disabled church.

These coming barbarians do not, however, have the future to themselves. *Jesus Christ the Lord is coming.* We know it not simply by a whisper in the wind; we know it by His Word. He came once; He comes again.

Jesus Christ the Lord is coming: the Lord of truth, to overwhelm all doubts. What hiding place then, when the God-who-is-there, Rewarder of all that diligently seek Him, acts to judge the secrets of men? What hiding place then for the big lie that dialectical materialism fully explains the whole of reality, for those who say the supernatural is but a myth? What hiding place then for God-is-dead buffoons, when the living God who declares man to be dead in trespasses and sins calls these dead to judgment? What hiding place then for God-may-be-alive theorists, when the self-revealing God asks what men have done with the truth of revelation? What hiding place then for God-is-only-love religionists, when the Lord who desires truth in the inward parts asks whether men have obeyed the truth? Jesus Christ the Lord of truth is coming: we know it by His Word.

Jesus Christ the Lord is coming: the King of kings, to overpower all reluctant powers. What hiding place then for totalitarian tyrants when at the name of Jesus every knee shall bow and every tongue confess that Jesus Christ is Lord (Phil 2:10-11)? What hiding place then for the nations East or West who trust in atomic stockpiles? What hiding place then for Israel or Arab powers spilling their blood for holy land

and holy city while the holy One of Israel still hangs crucified outside the gates? What hiding place then for heathen nations still mired in darkness, and for Gentile nations whose scorn of God is a scandal to the pagan world? Jesus Christ the King of kings is coming: we know it by His Word.

Jesus Christ the Lord is coming: the man of righteousness, to overflow the grace of God, but to override all scorners. He returns and overturns. In the final resurrection of the dead He overturns the whole human race. Those who reject Him, He turns to rout and everlasting separation; those who love Him, He turns fully into the holy image of God. He comes to vindicate the righteousness of God and to crown the grace of God. Jesus Christ the Lord of life and Lord of all—of creation life, of redemption life, of resurrection life—is coming. Jesus Christ our Lord is coming: we know it by His Word.

The barbarians are coming; the Lord Jesus Christ is coming. *Christians are here now; do they know whether they are coming or going?*

To the world we seem like Hogan's army waiting for Godot. Can we take a holy initiative in history? Can we once more strike an apostolic stride? Can we put an ungodly world on the defensive again? Can we show men the folly of opposing Him who has already overcome the world, of rejecting fellowship with the coming King? Will we offer civilization a realistic option, or only a warning of impending doom? Will Christianity speak only to man's fears and frustrations, or will it also fill the vacuum in his heart and crown his longings for life at its best?

Unless evangelical Christians break out of their cultural isolation, unless we find new momentum in the modern world, we may find ourselves so much on the margin of the stream of modern history that by 1975 ours will be virtually a Dead Sea caves community. Our supposed spiritual vitality will be known only to ourselves, and publicly we will be laughed at as quaint but obsolescent.

Institutional Christianity is already in very deep trouble. Liberal theology has only a political importance now, and even here its marriage to the god of revolution begets no criterion for distinguishing the divine from the demonic. Future historians may well look back upon our own lifetime as that very point in church history when the Christian churches forfeited their greatest spiritual opportunity since the apostolic age. We make a fetish of church union, devote millions upon millions of dollars to ecclesiastical administration and buildings, sound an unclear gospel from a blurred Bible, debate the task of Christianity in the mass media and, all the while, lose evangelistic momentum.

The Christian church is here with a global mandate and a Great Commission. Will the multitudes in the streets hear a stirring in the wind and sense afresh that Pentecost is blowing our way? Will they recognize that a new option does remain for individuals and for the human race?

The church of Jesus Christ is here. We must march and sing our faith again in the public arena—in the streets and on the mass media—not hide our light under church buildings and inside seminary walls. It was in the open marketplace that the apostle Paul engaged Stoic and Epicurean philosophers in debate.

God's commandments need once again to become an issue in national life, the truth of revelation a matter of importance in every sphere of modern culture, the call for social righteousness a cause for trembling in every vale of injustice. Neither modern scientists nor modern historians stand a ghost of a chance of burying and bolting Jesus of Nazareth in a Palestinian tomb unless we shroud Him through our silence, unless we keep quiet about the sure future toward which He is guiding all history.

The church often tells the world where it is going; does the church today any longer know where she is going? The church of Jesus Christ is here and has her marching orders;

our mandate is His Word. Everything else around us is on the move; have we opted out of the contest for the mind and will and heart of modern man?

The church of Jesus Christ is here—not white or black, not West or East, not denominational or nondenominational, but transracial, transnational, transdenominational. Breaking down our fences, we must link hands and hearts with Christian believers of every race and region in a common thrust for evangelical faith in evangelism, education, and social involvement. If while evangelizing we abandon education to alien philosophies, we shall abet a climate that condemns Christianity as a religion for anti-intellectuals only. We shall veil the fact that the reasons given for modern unbelief are invalid rationalizations. We shall obscure the truth that evangelical theism involves a compelling intellectual commitment.

If while evangelizing we abandon the sociopolitical realm to its own devices, we shall fortify the misimpression that the public order falls wholly outside the command and will of God. We shall foster the erroneous belief that Christianity deals with private concerns only and conceal the fact that government exists by God's will as His servant for the sake of justice and order. Wherever man's distress threatens his humanity, the church of Christ has something desperately relevant to say and is wholly obliged to say it. Let the church remain silent about it, and even some pagans will respond as Christians ought to, while others will exploit the valleys of discontent for political advantage or their own personal benefit.

But if we seek to capture men's minds, and struggle for just social structures, yet neglect the evangelization of the earth, we shall fail our generation where it needs help most of all. Walter Lippman has ventured to answer his own question of "whether anything can be done soon enough to cope with the problems before they engulf us," by saying: "It isn't that it's

beyond human nature's capacity to do it; it's that human nature is so lazy and selfish and often corrupt that it doesn't do
it."

Malcolm Muggeridge recently put it: "The most extra-
ordinary thing about human beings" is "that they pursue ends
which they know to be disastrous and turn their backs on
ways which they know to be joyous." Do we not see that
what's wrong with modern man is precisely what the apostolic church diagnosed as the root of the problem of fallen man
everywhere: a sinful heart that does not love God and neighbor? No stocking of the mind, no altering of the environment, will effect the full change that God demands: "Ye must
be born again. . . . Except a man be born again, he cannot
see the kingdom of God" (Jn 3:7, 3).

The church of Jesus Christ is here, mandated with a mission personal and public, a mission transdenominational,
transnational, transcultural; our mandate is His Word.

The church of Jesus Christ is here: in a world halting between pseudo-lords and the Lord of lords, here with a specific message to proclaim. She is entrusted with God's truth,
not with man-made theories. The late twentieth century is
bone-weary of the indefinite and inconclusive and indecisive;
what it needs is a sure Word of God. A church that forsakes
the truth of revelation soon yields to the detouring modernity
of the youngsters or to the crippling tradition of the elders,
and will "teach as doctrines the commandments of men"
(Mk 7:7, NEB).

The coming barbarians have no real future; neither has a
church that forsakes the truth of God. The Word of God is
given, incarnate and incomparable, inscripturate and indeli-
ble. That God has revealed Himself intelligibly, that Jesus
of Nazareth is the incarnate Logos of God, that the Scriptures are the Word of God written, that the Holy Spirit uses
the truth of God as the means of human persuasion and conviction, that not even the twentieth century can cancel God's
truth, that the Word of God is not bound, but that all who

neglect it are in a tragic bind—these are emphases our generation needs desperately to hear.

"Thus saith the Lord!" is the only barricade that can save our unheeding generation from inevitable calamity. When all is said and tried, modern man's alternatives are either a return to the truth of revelation or an ever deeper plunge into meaninglessness and loss of worth.

In the twilight traffic snarl of a great civilization, the church needs to be light to the world and to shelter the moral fortunes of human history from crippling collision. To hold the road for Jesus Christ requires authoritative charting, clarity of vision, and divine enabling. The church is here at the crossroads. Open the Bible again; our mandate is His Word. The church is here—called to be a living exposition of the truth of revelation.

The barbarians are coming; the Lord Jesus Christ is coming; let the church that is here come *now*, with good news, with the only durable good news, and come in time!

Notes

CHAPTER 2

1. Joseph Fletcher, *Situation Ethics* (Philadelphia: Westminster, 1966), p. 140.

CHAPTER 3

1. Donald MacKinnon, *Borderlands of Theology* (London: Lutterworth, 1968), p. 51.
2. Ibid., p. 53.
3. Malcolm Muggeridge, article in *Anglican World* (London) 8, no. 36 (1968): 49.

CHAPTER 4

1. Edmund Leach, *A Runaway World?* (London: BBC, 1968).
2. Ibid., pp. 48, 56.
3. Ibid., p. 49.
4. Ibid., p. 47.
5. Leach, "When Scientists Play the Role of God," *The Times* (London), Sept. 16, 1968.
6. Ibid.
7. Leach, *A Runaway World?* p. 59.
8. Leach, "When Scientists Play. . . ."
9. Ibid.
10. Leach, *A Runaway World?*, pp. 31, 84.
11. Ibid., p. 35.
12. Ibid., p. 90.
13. Ibid., pp. 31 f.
14. Ibid., p. 18.

CHAPTER 5

1. Gordon H. Clark, *Religion, Reason and Revelation* (Philadelphia: Presbyterian & Reformed, 1961), p. 6.
2. L. W. Grensted, *The Psychology of Religion* (New York: Oxford U., 1952), p. 15.
3. Clark, pp. 22-23.

CHAPTER 7

1. Rollo May, *Man's Search for Himself* (New York: Norton, 1953), p. 14.
2. *Look* magazine, Oct. 29, 1968.

CHAPTER 9

1. Gordon Taylor, *Biological Time Bomb* (New York: Signet Books, 1969).
2. C. S. Lewis, *Miracles: A Preliminary Study* (New York: Macmillan, 1947), p. 172.
3. Cf. Van Austin Harvey, *The Historian and the Believer* (New York: Macmillan, 1967).

CHAPTER 10

1. John Updike, "Seven Stanzas at Easter" in *Telephone Poles and Other Poems* (New York: Knopf, 1961). Used by permission.

CHAPTER 11

1. James A. Michener, *The Quality of Life* (Philadelphia: Lippincott, 1970).

CHAPTER 15

1. W. A. Visser 't Hooft, *The Renewal of the Church* (Philadelphia: Westminster, 1956), p. 95.

CHAPTER 16

1. Russell Kirk, *Enemies of the Permanent Things* (New Rochelle, N.Y.: Arlington House, 1969).